ADULT COLORING BOOKS

# MANDALAS

# &

# FLOWERS

Lilly Addison

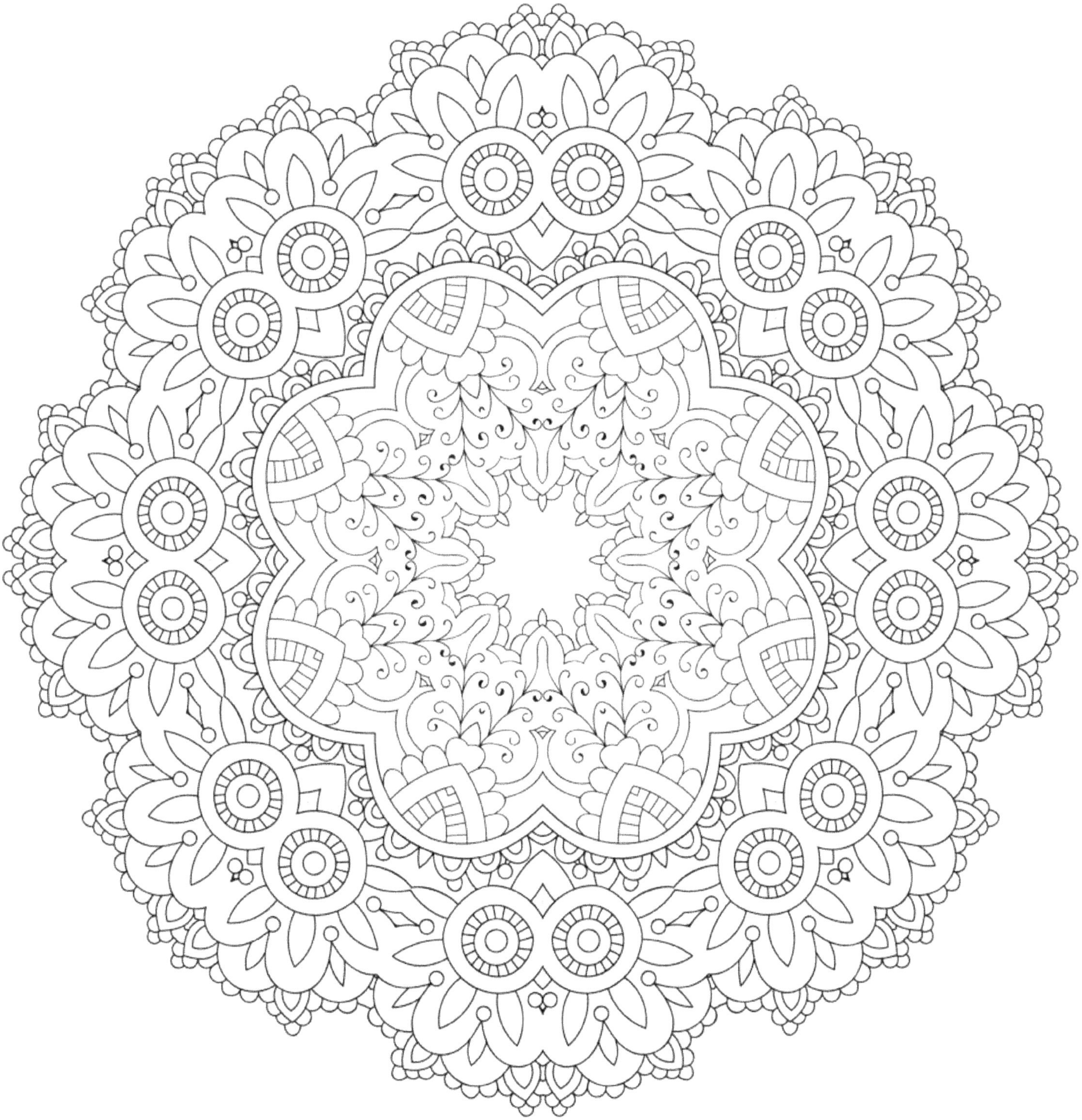

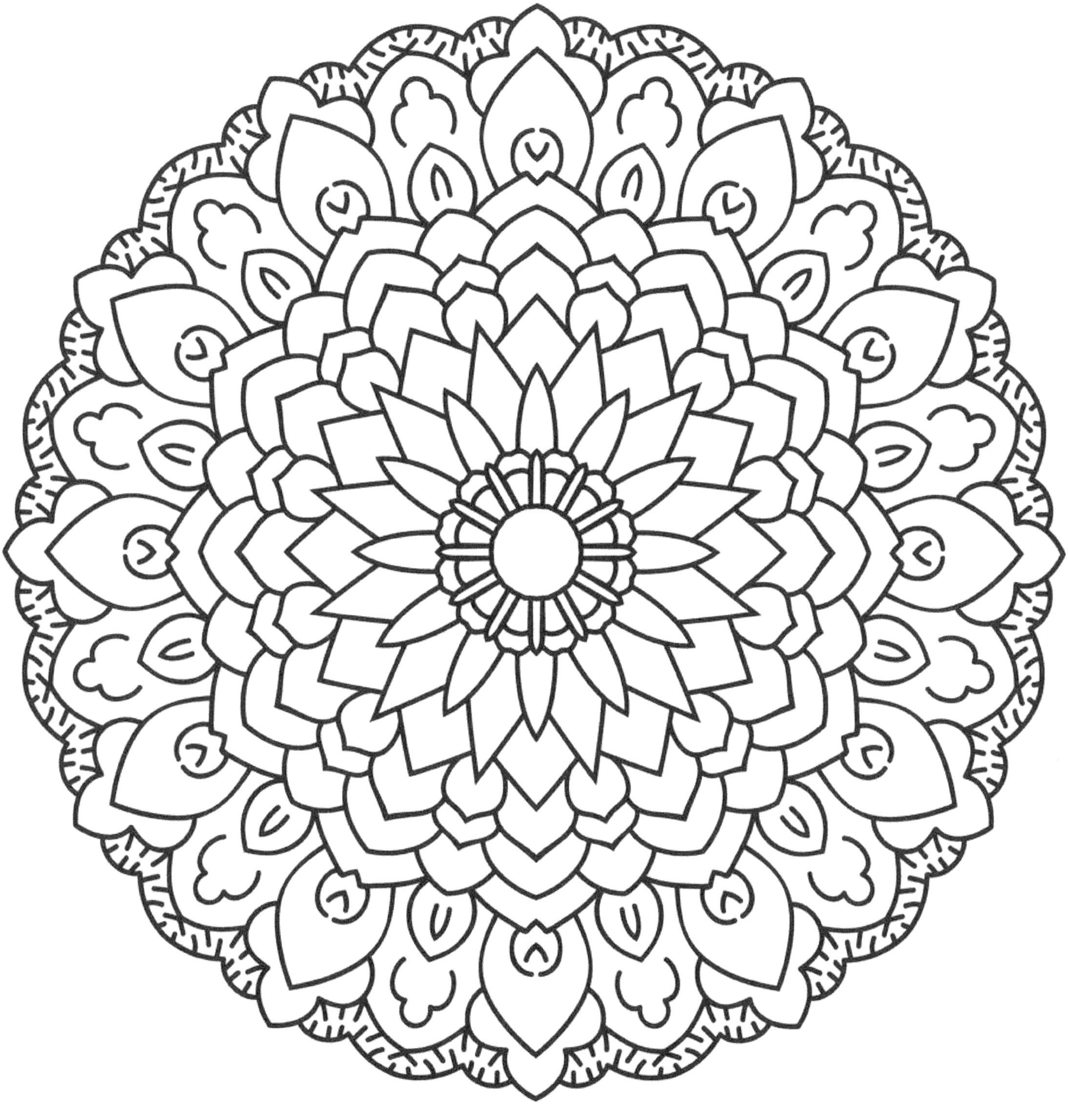

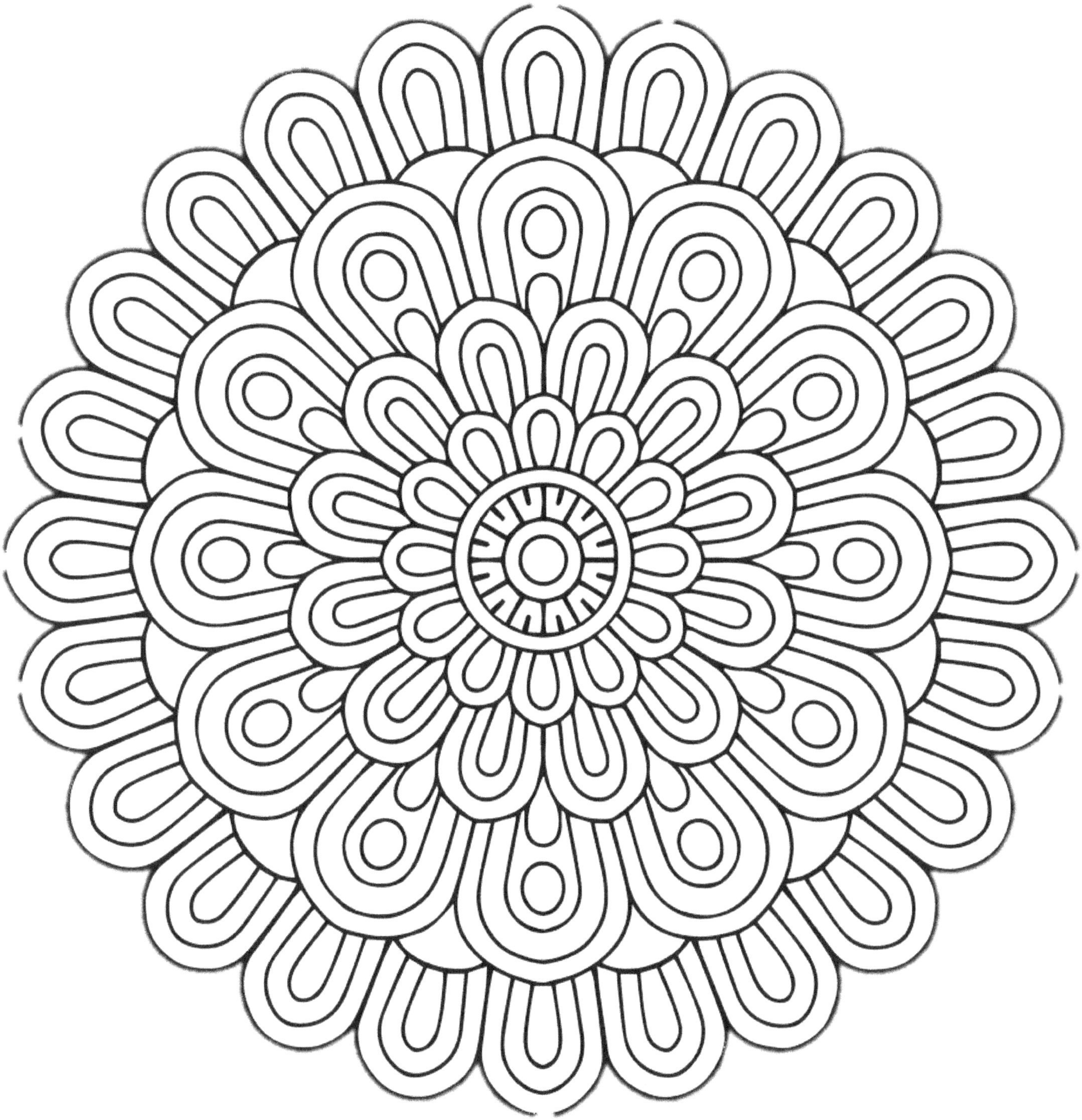

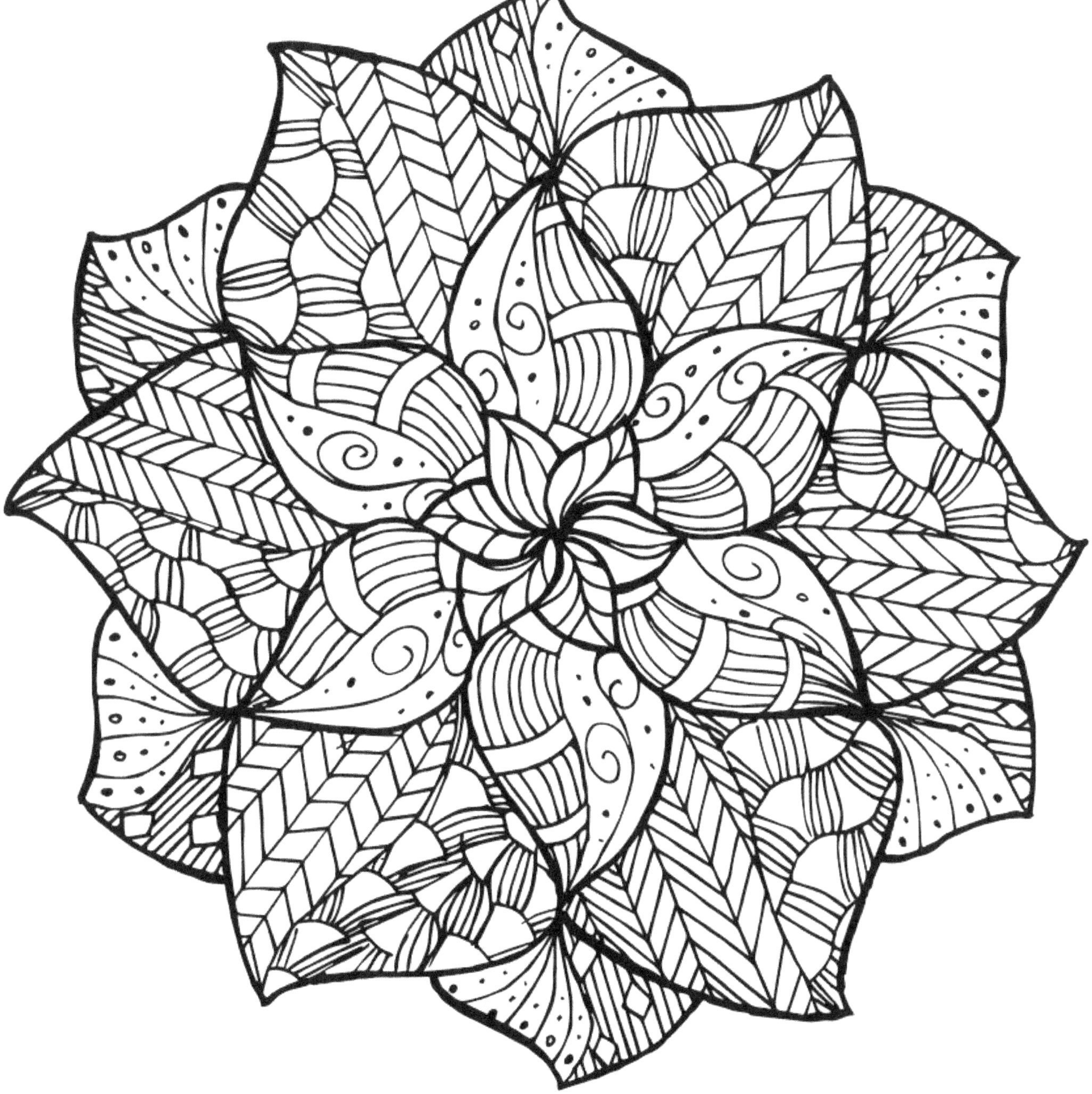

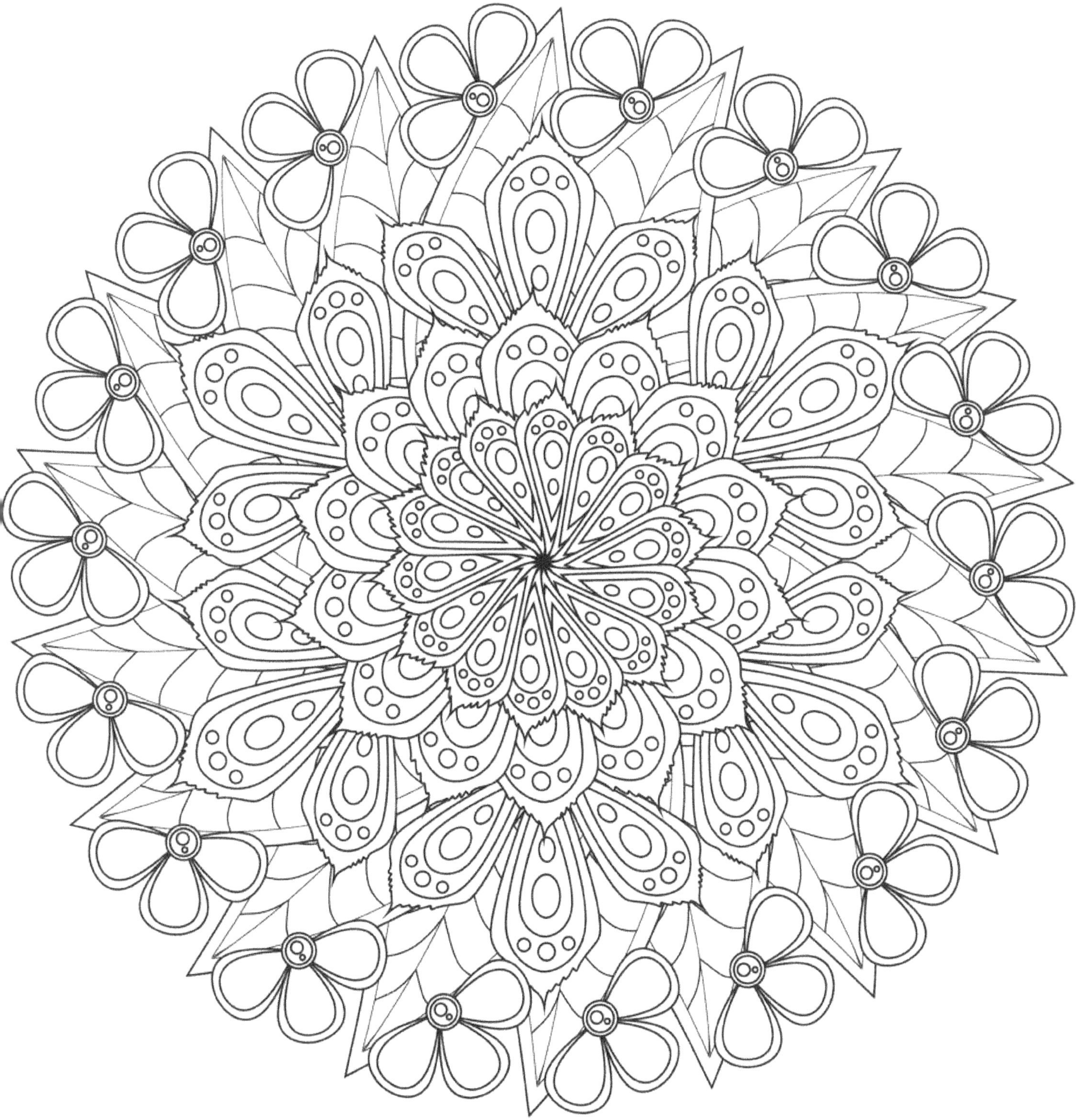

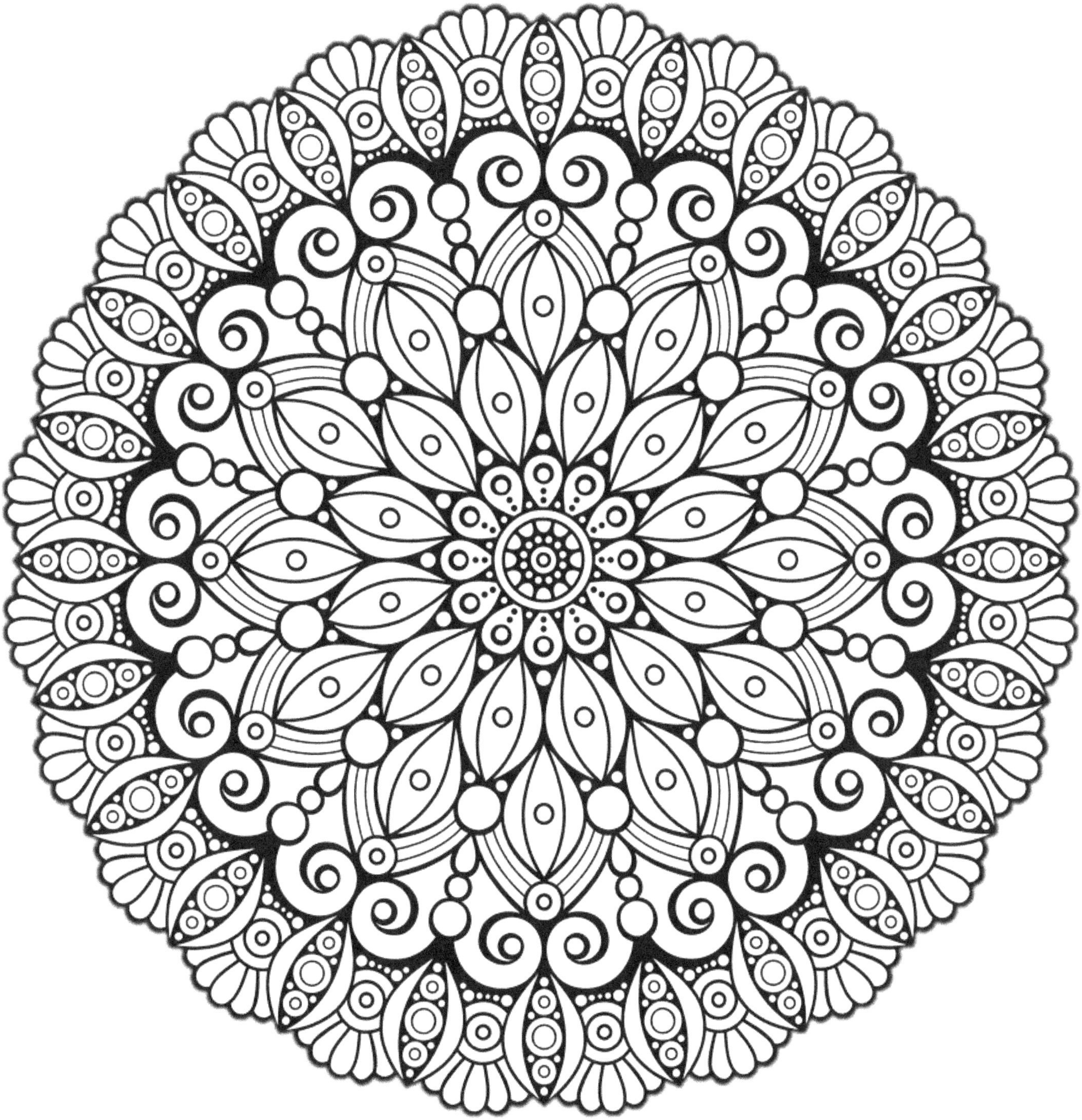

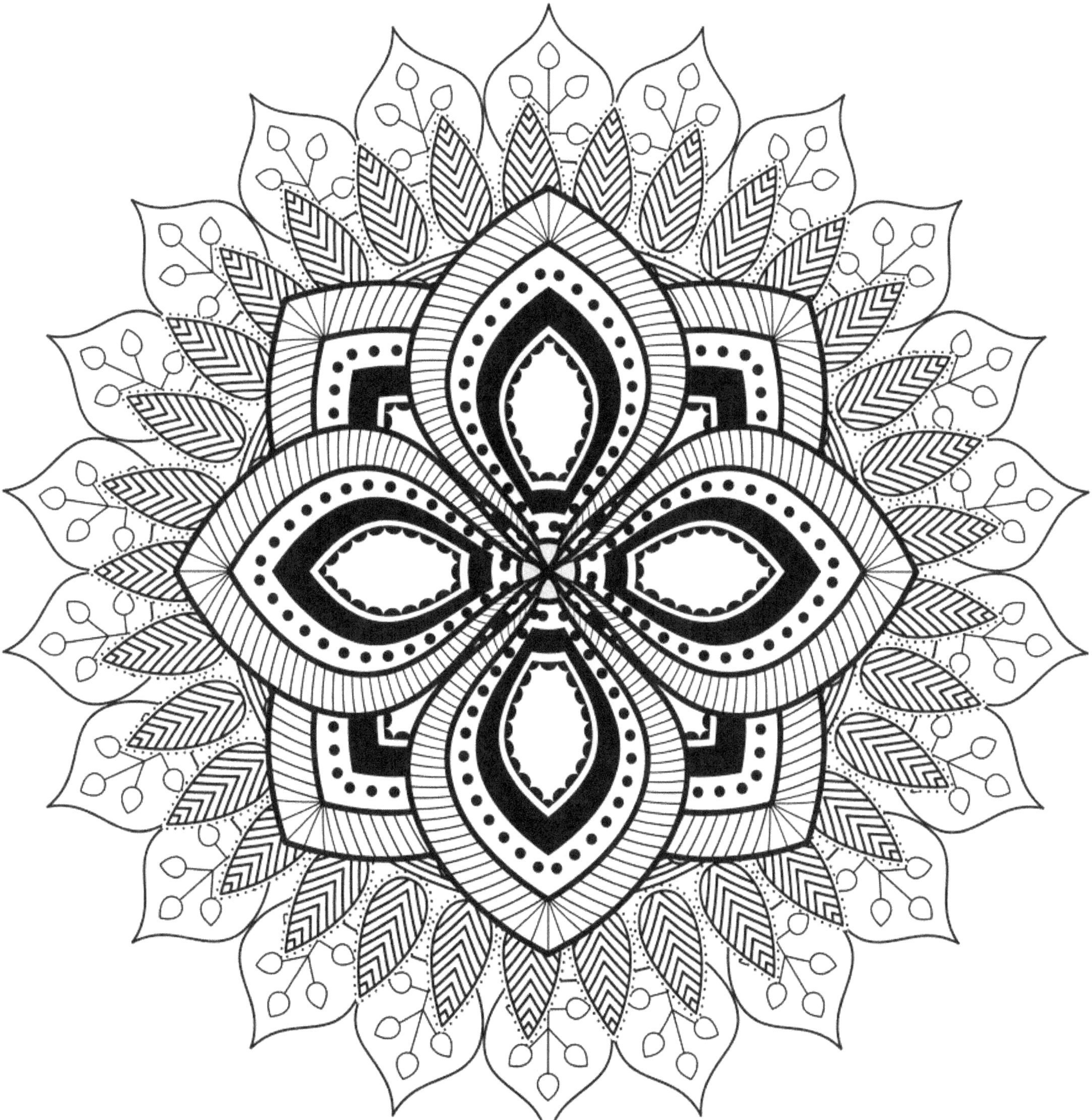

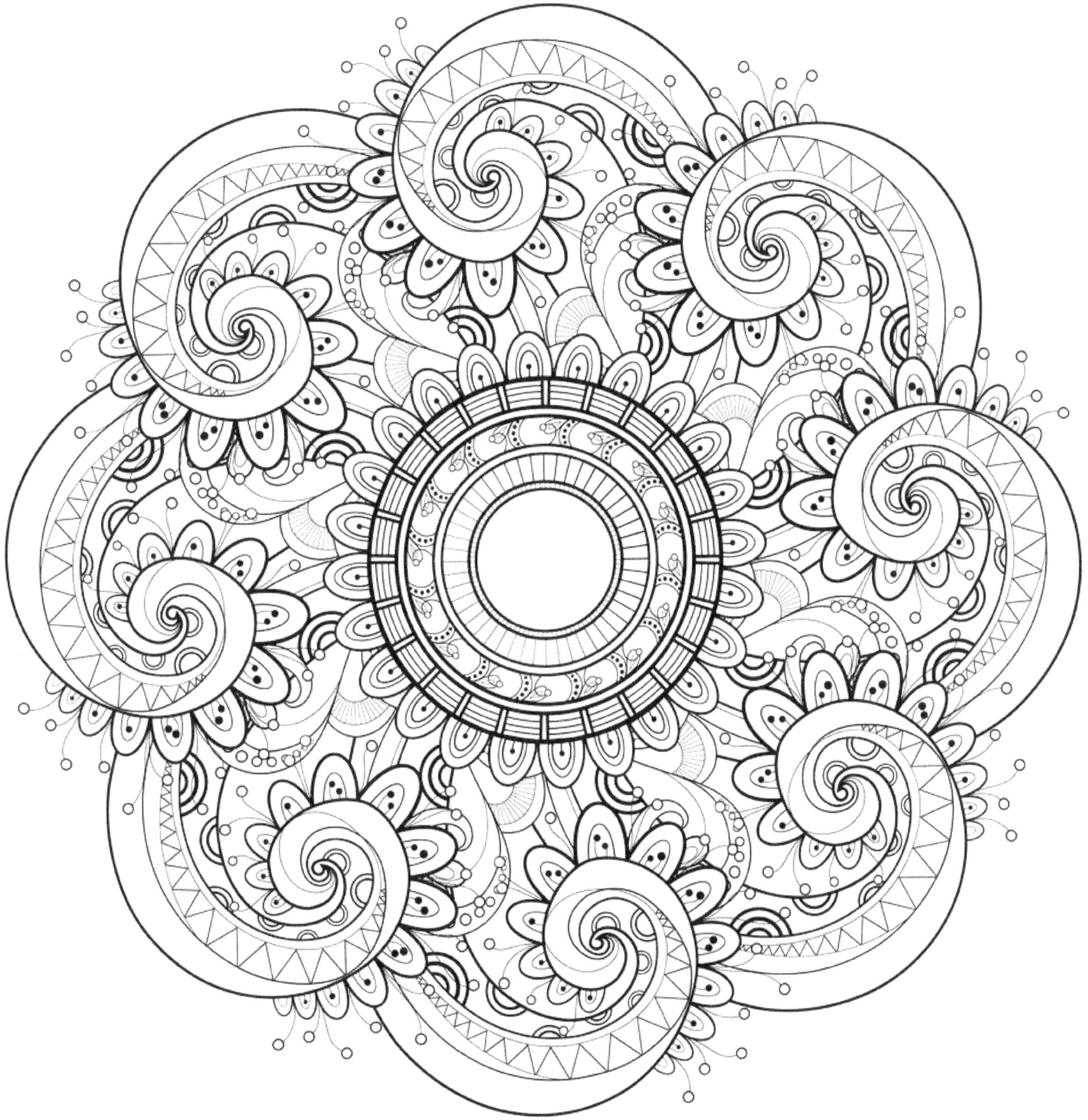

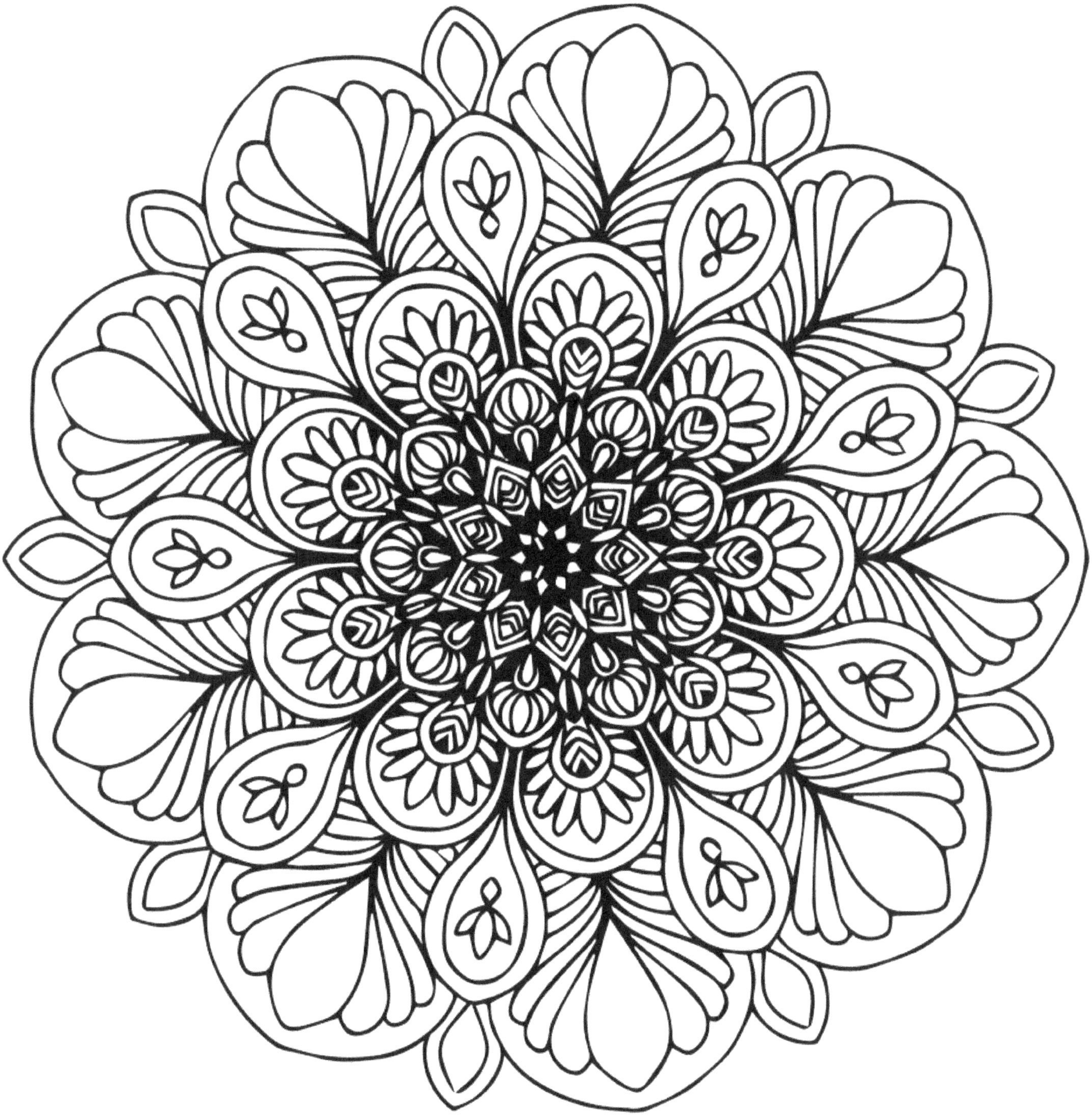

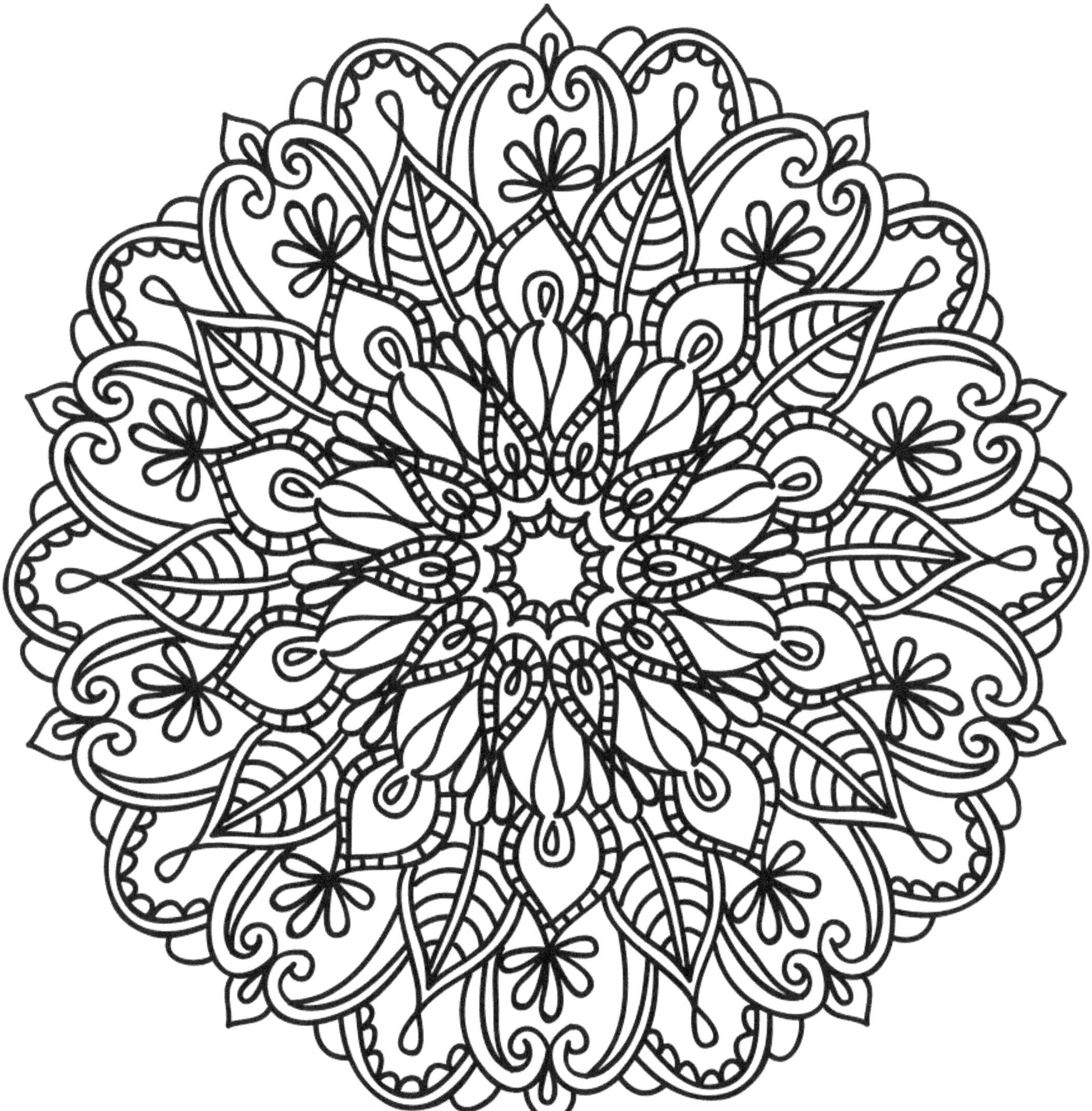

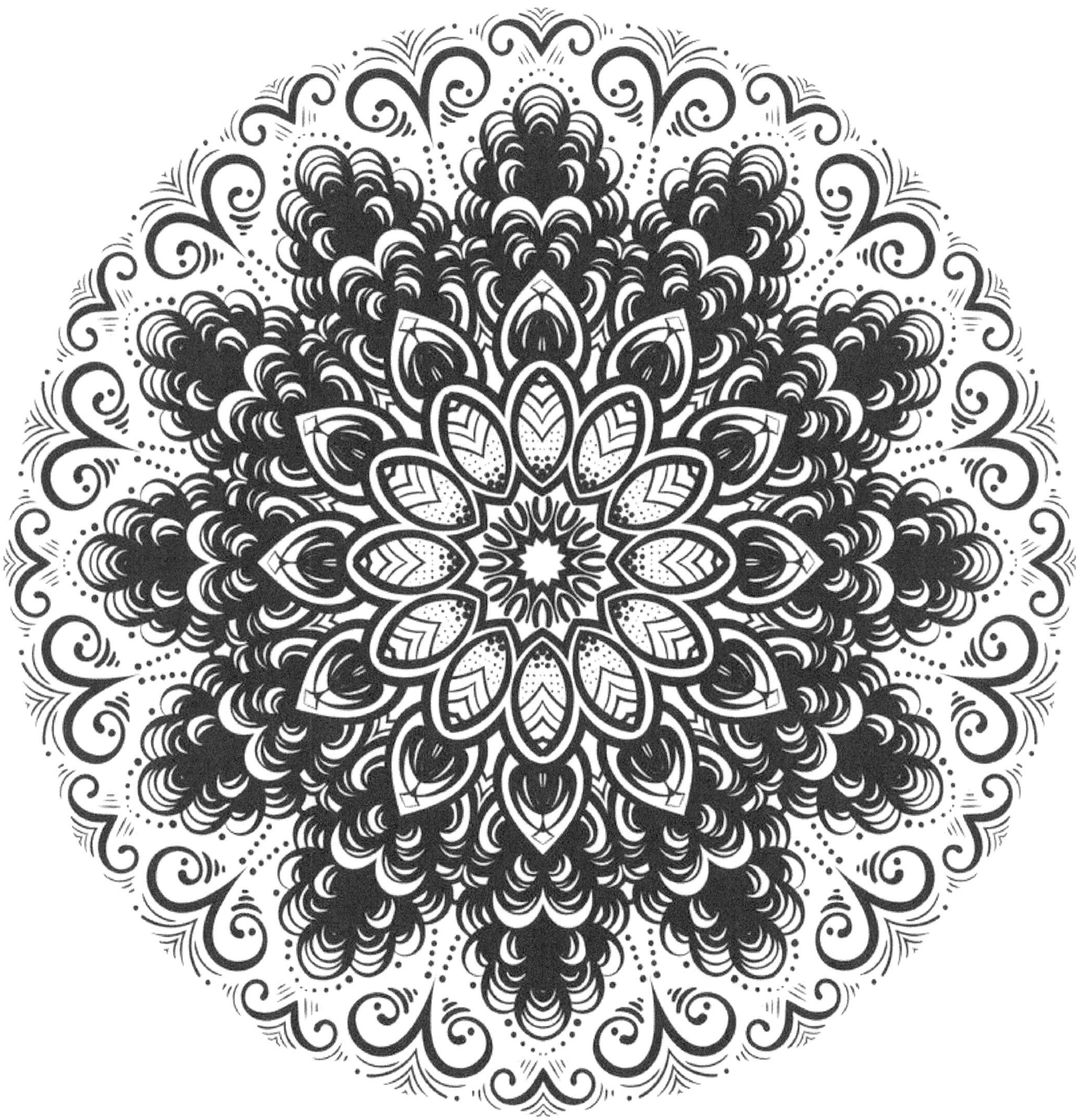

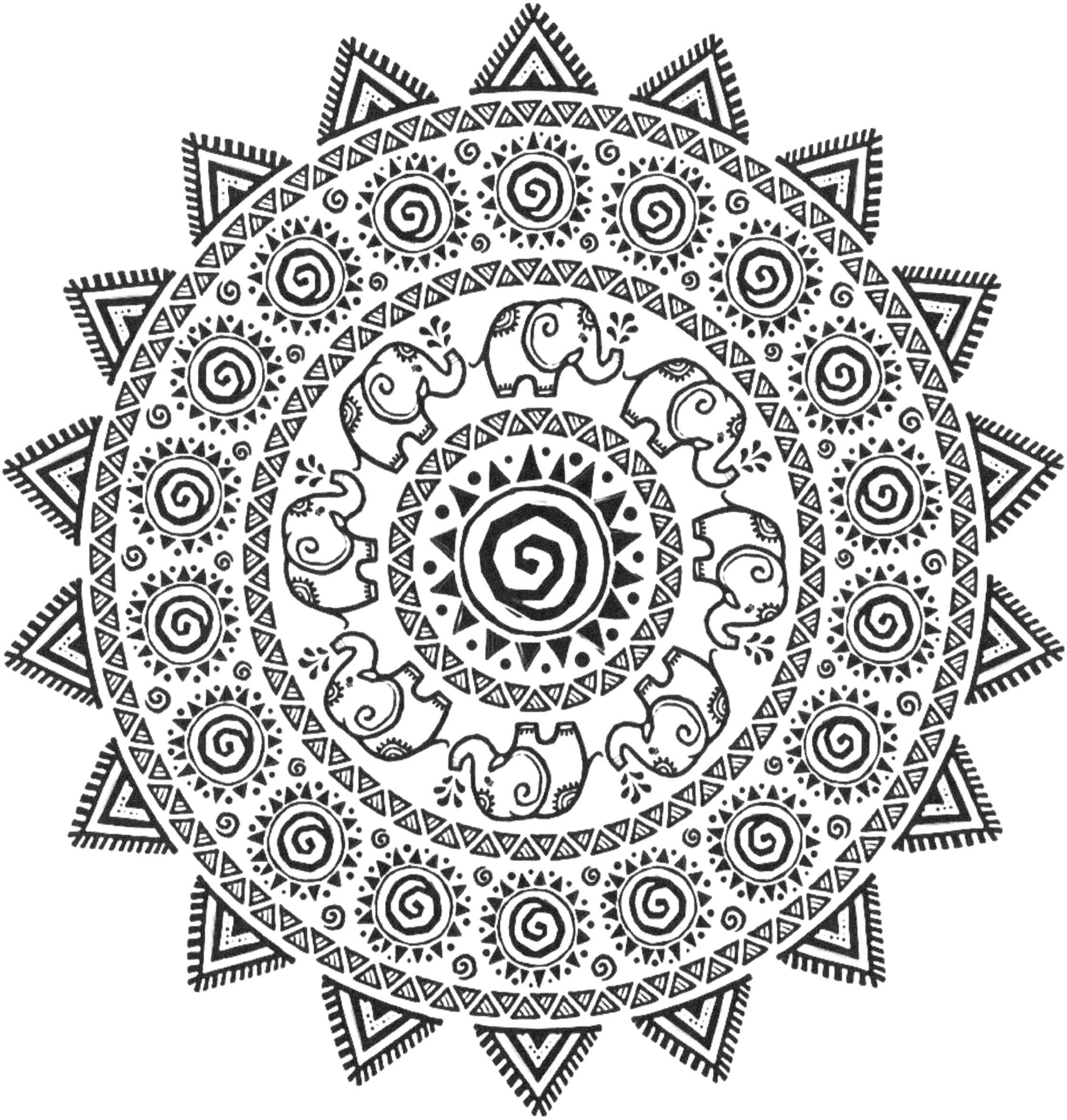

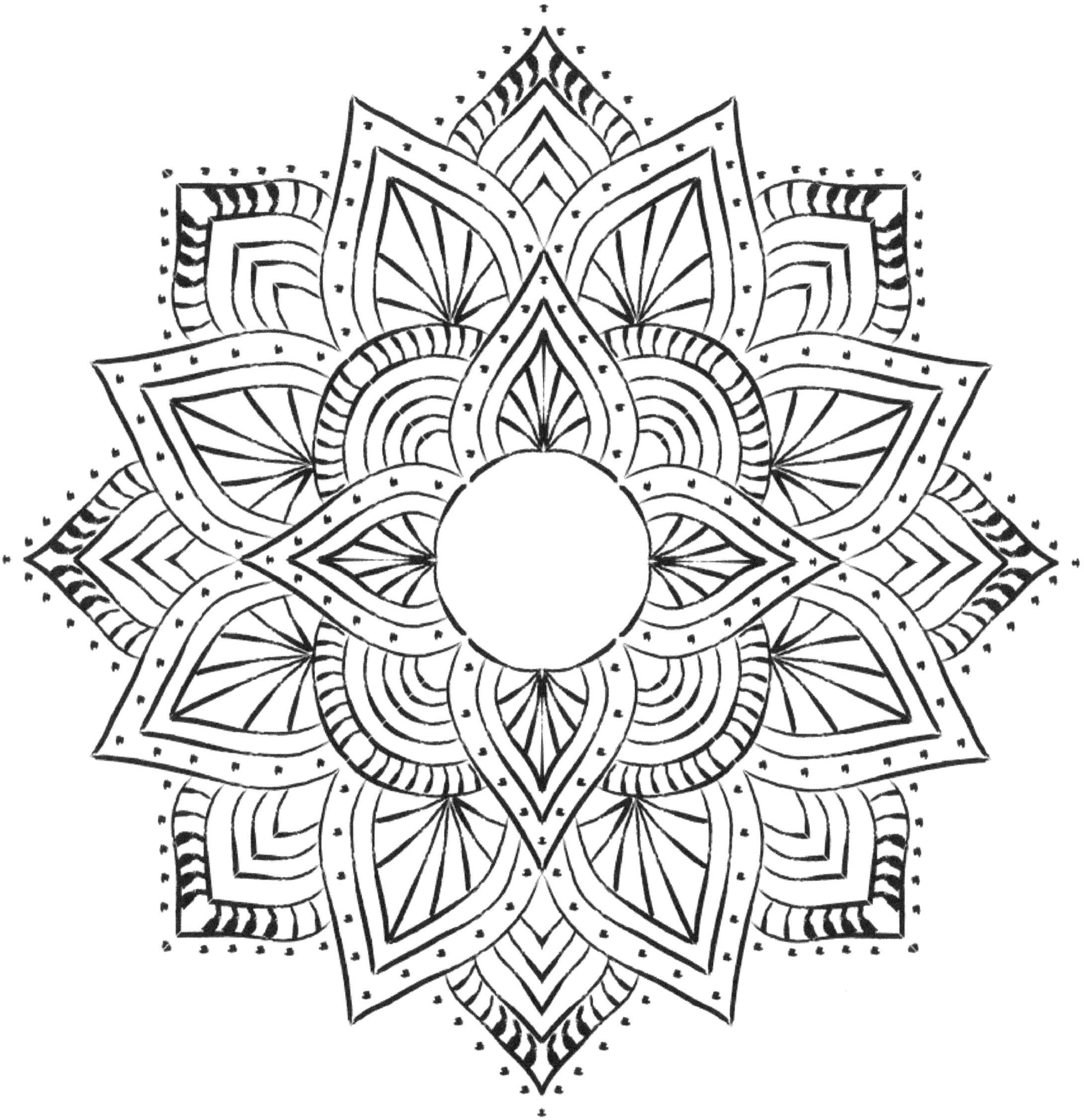

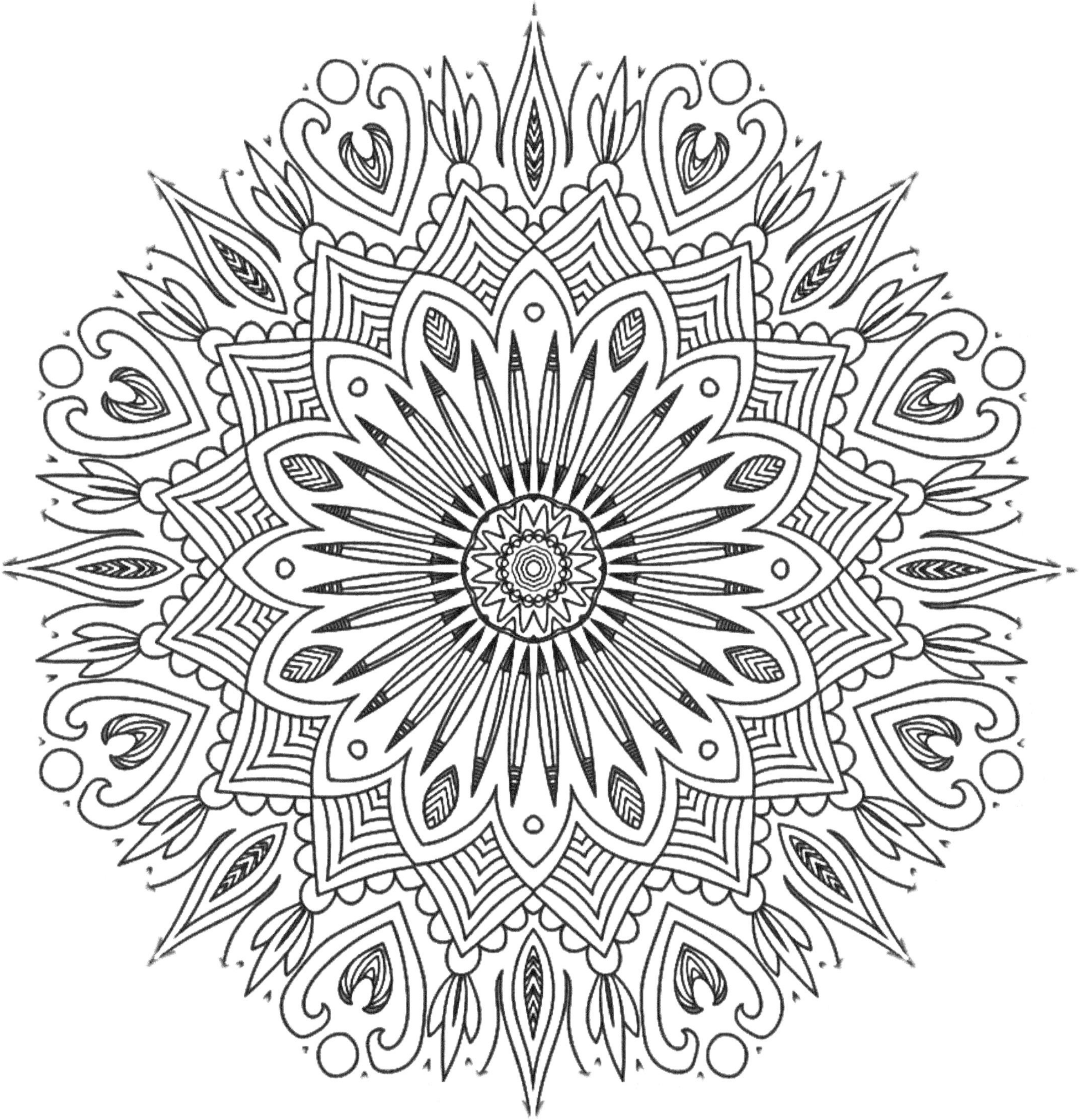

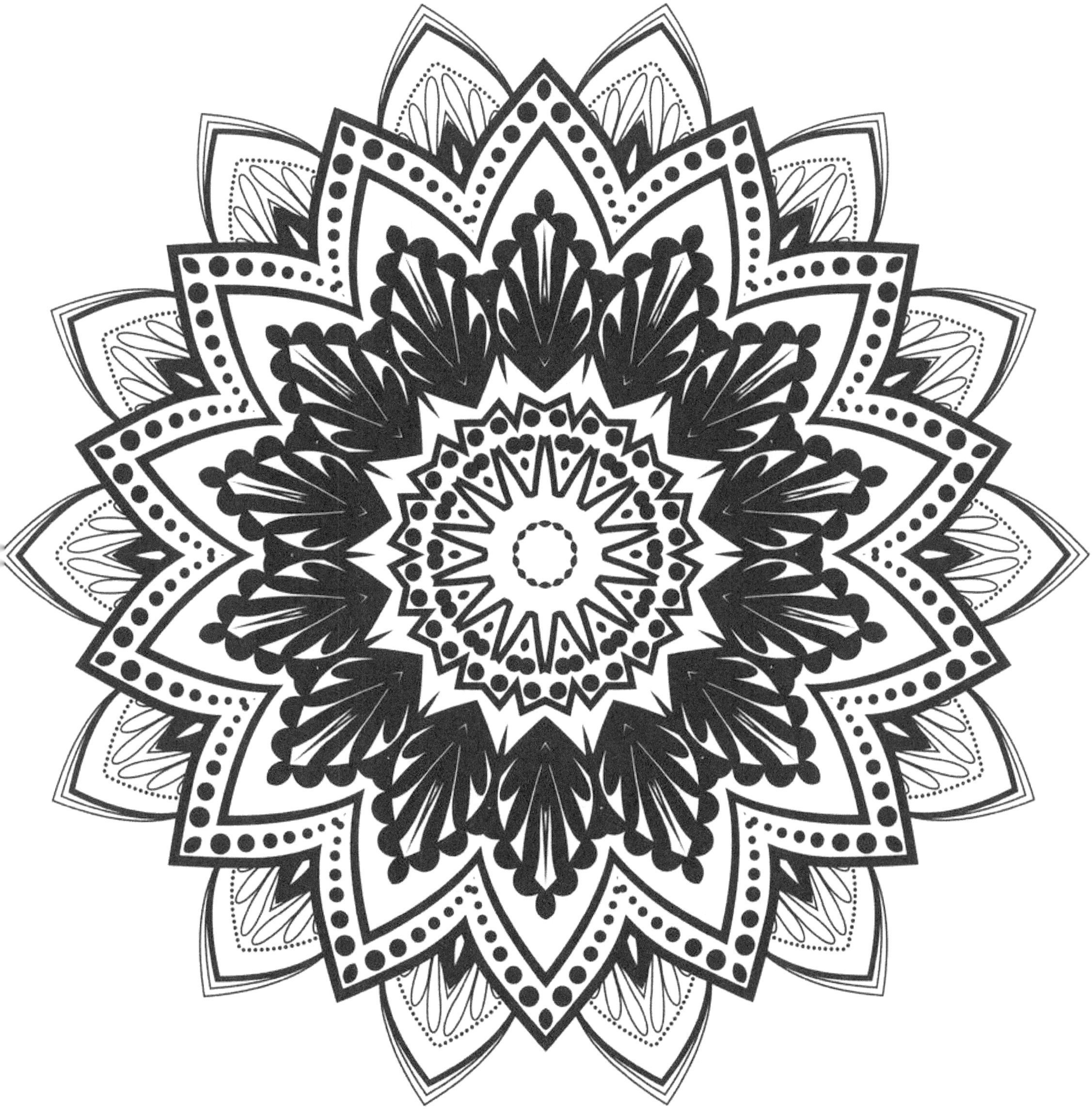

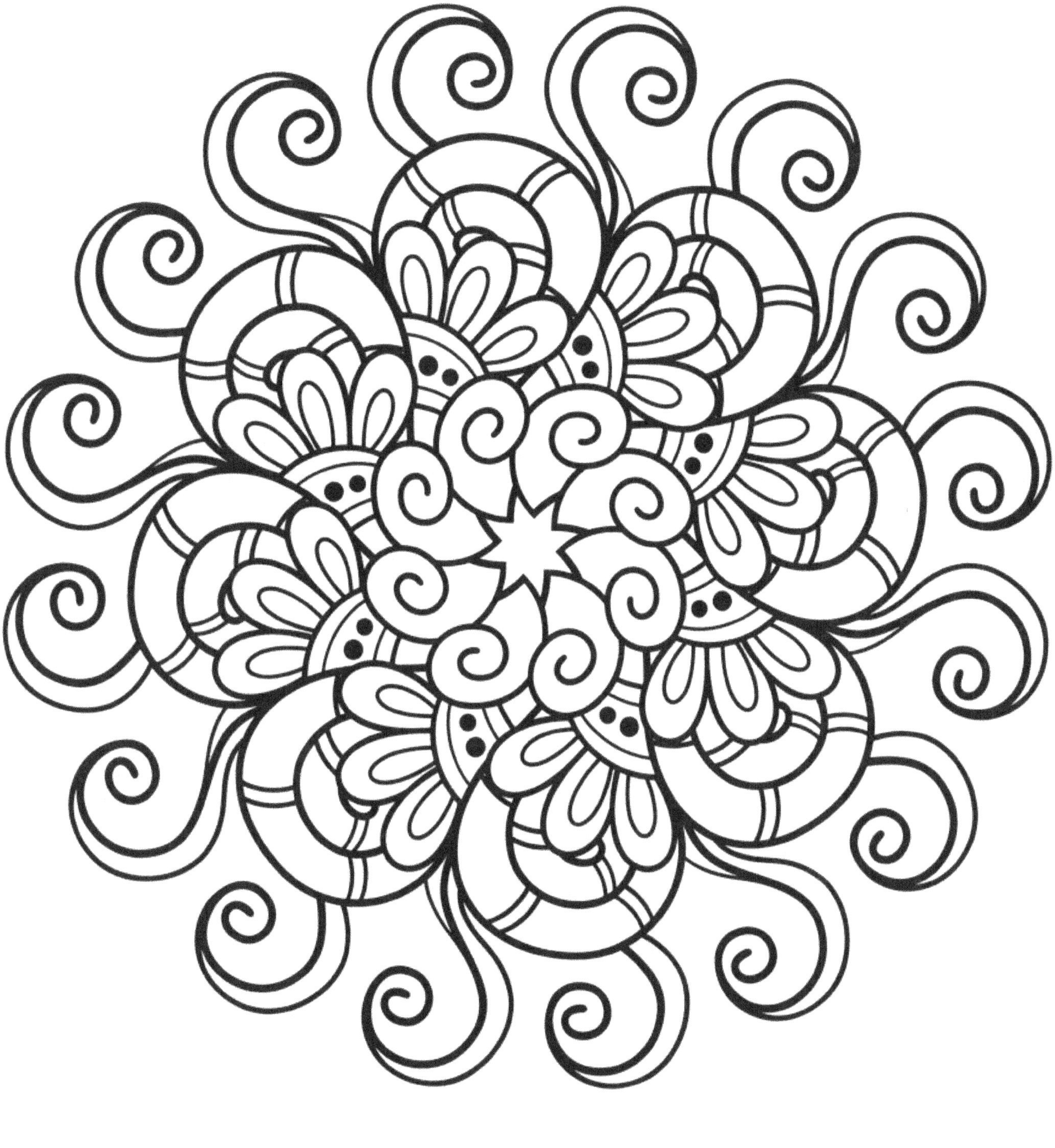

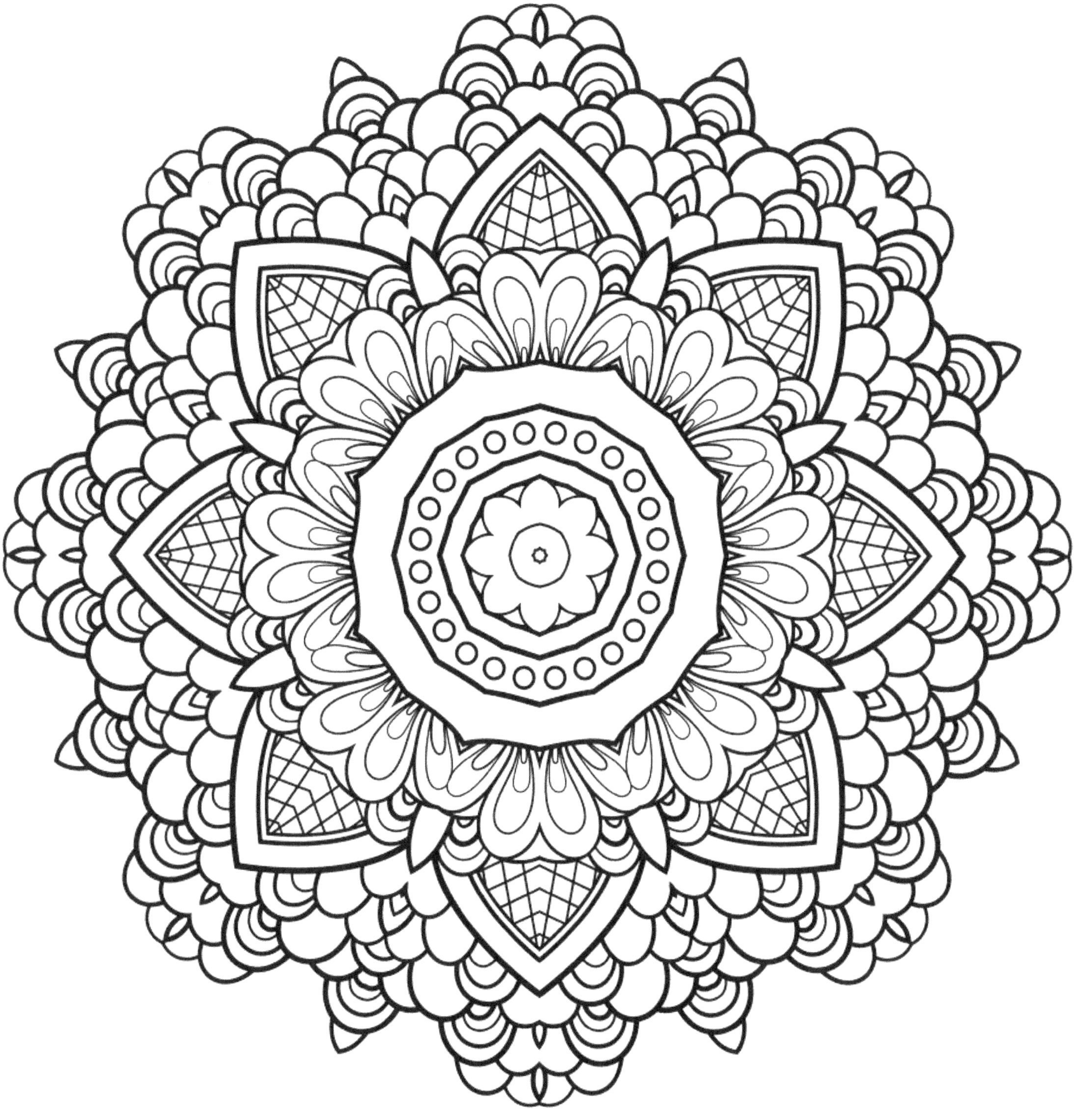

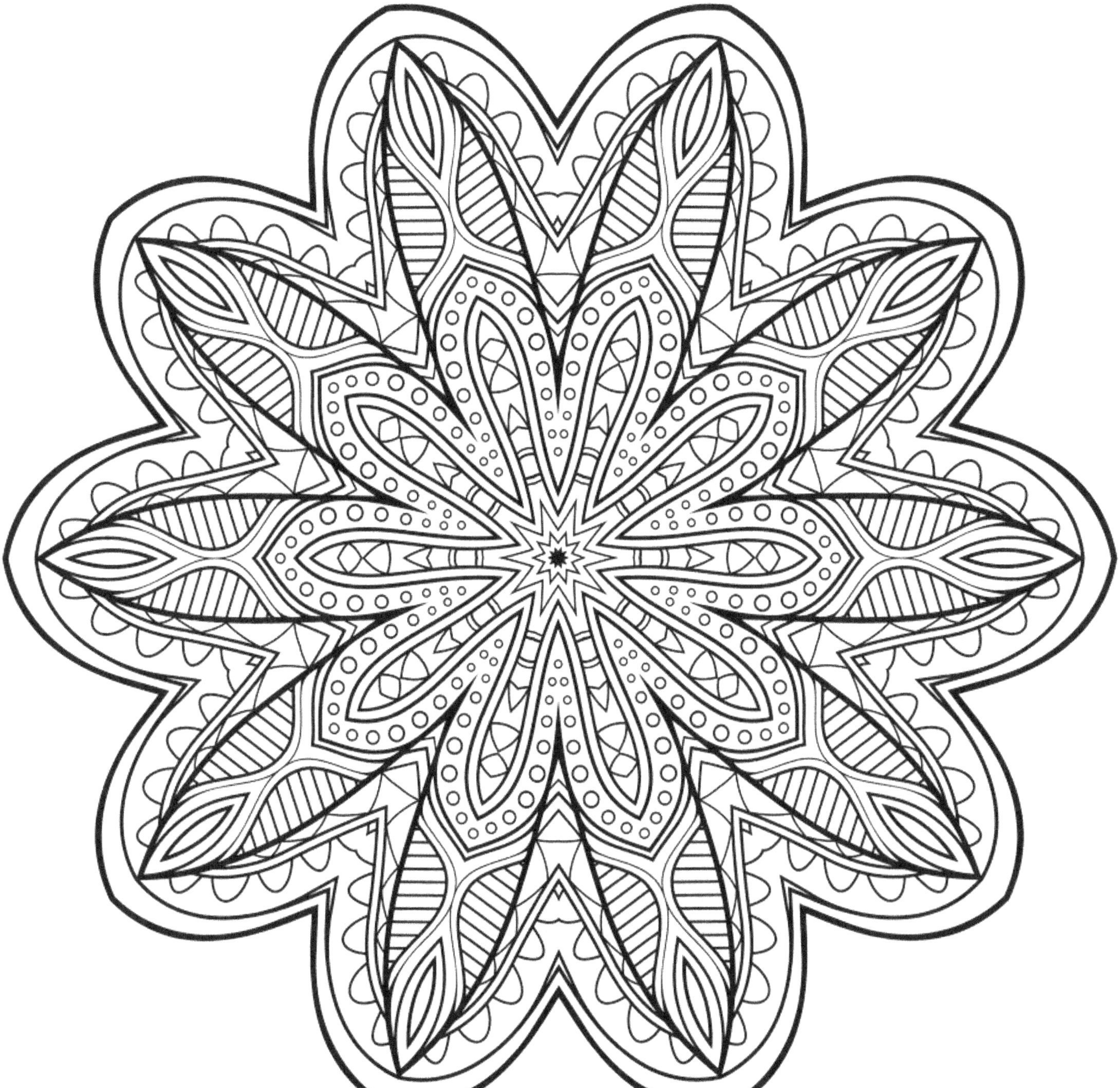

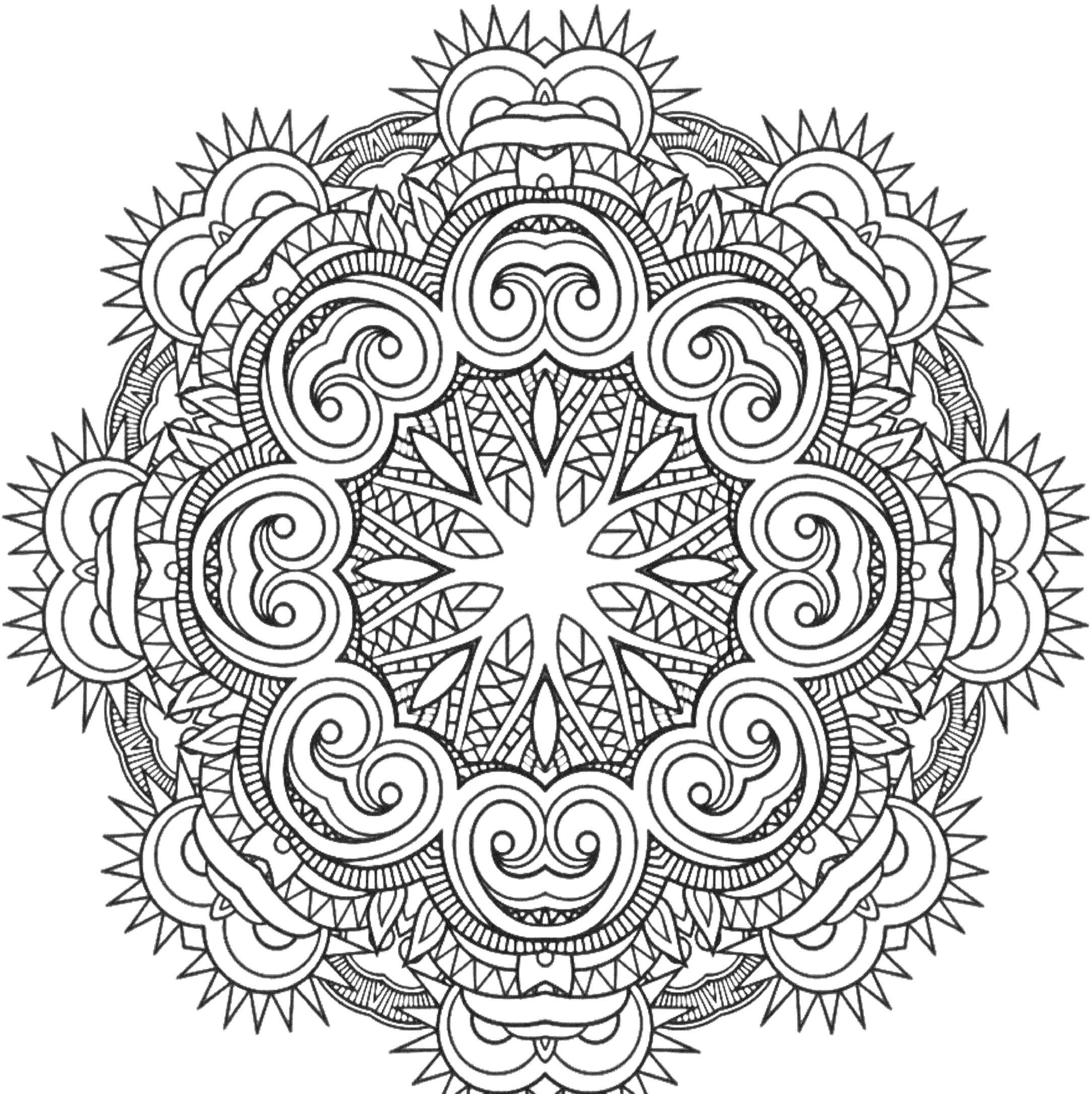

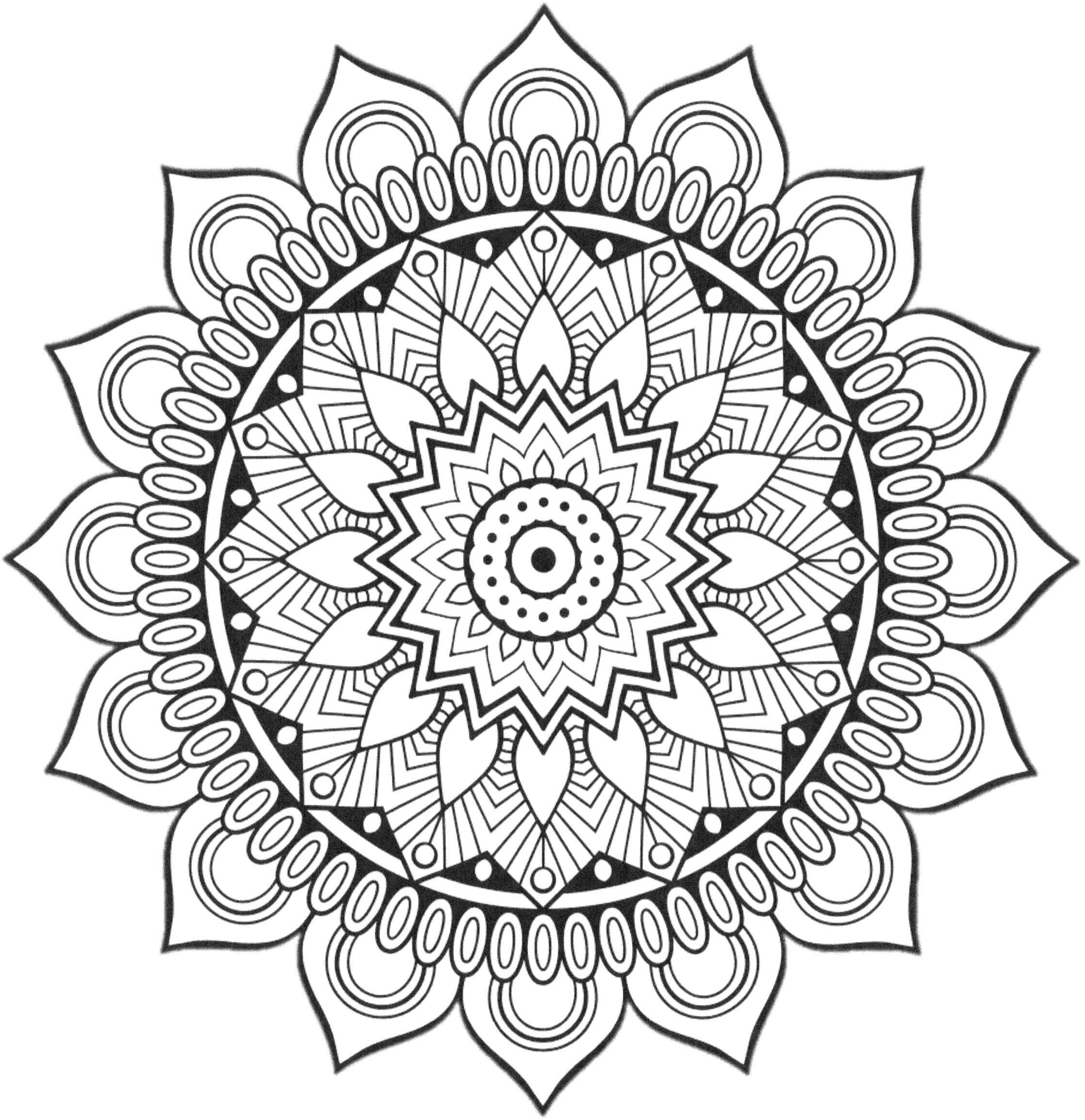

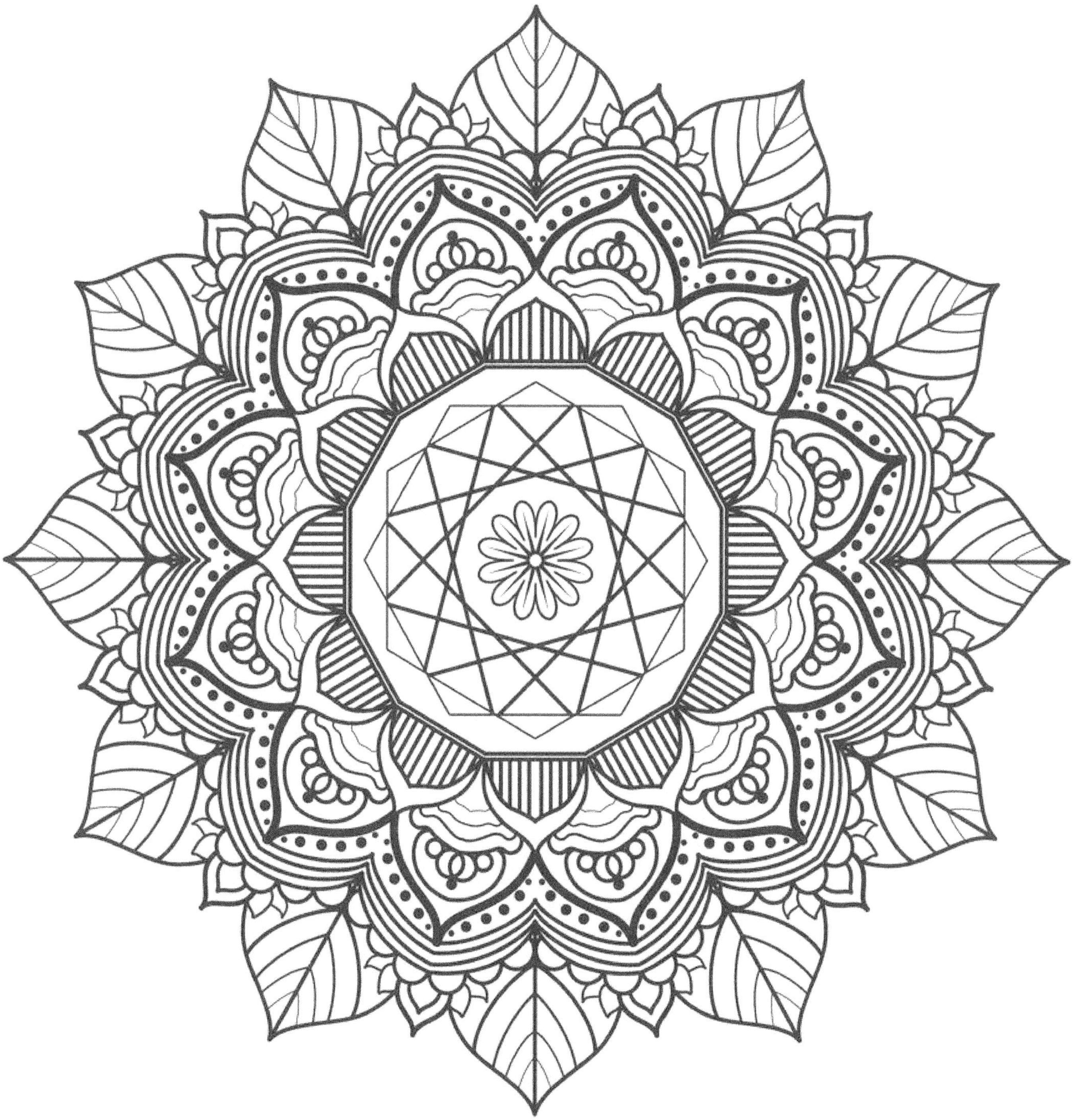

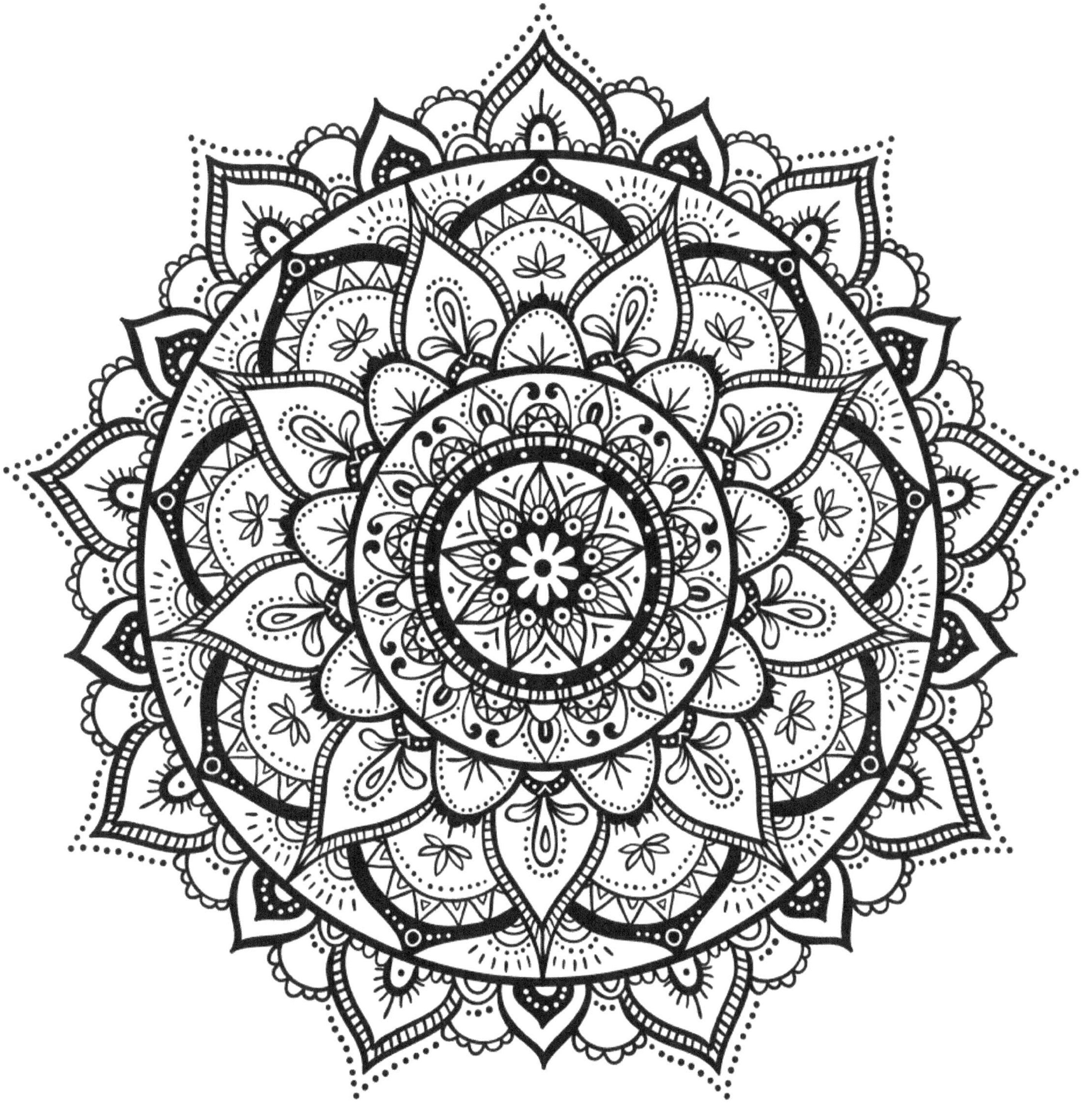

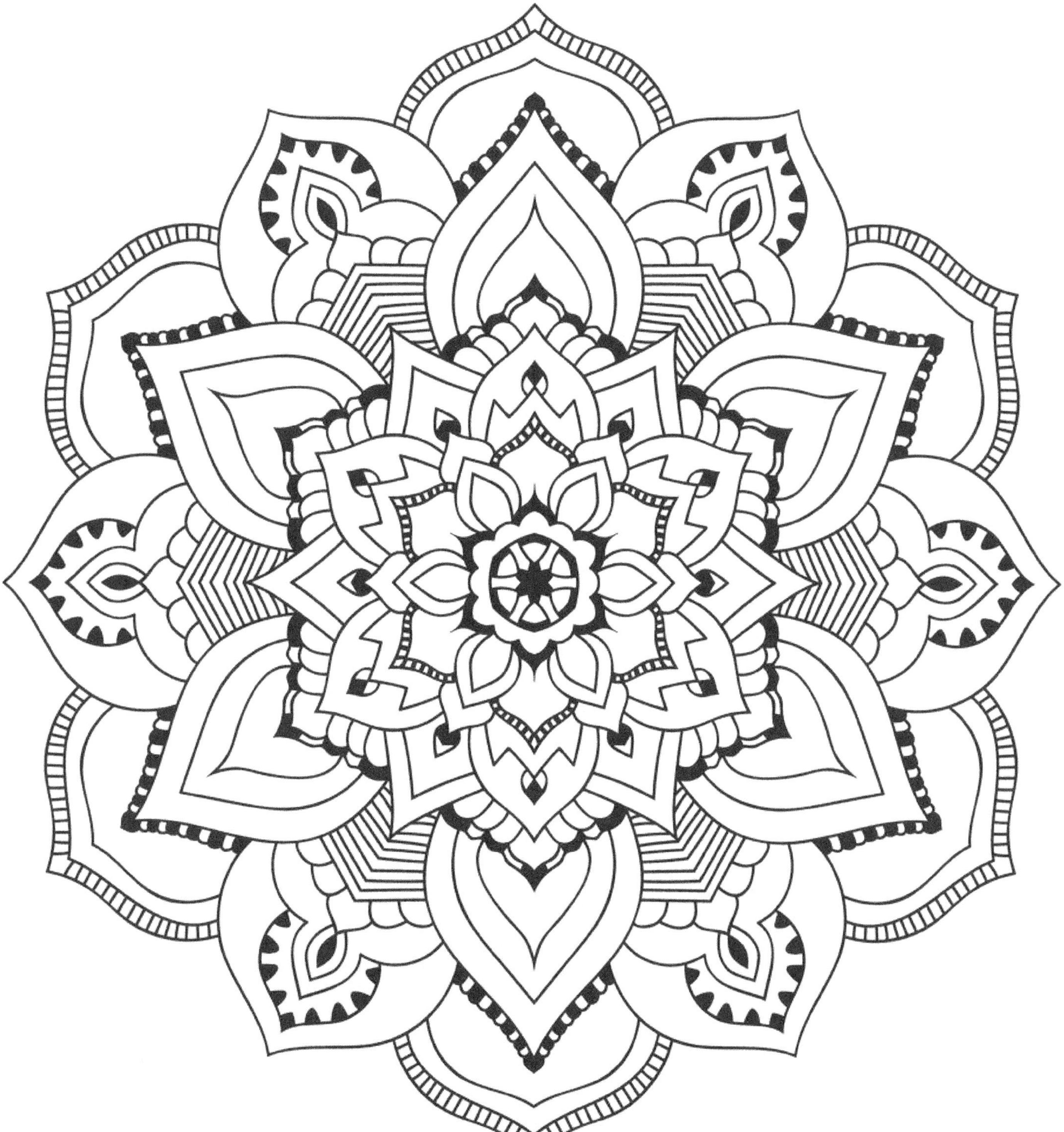

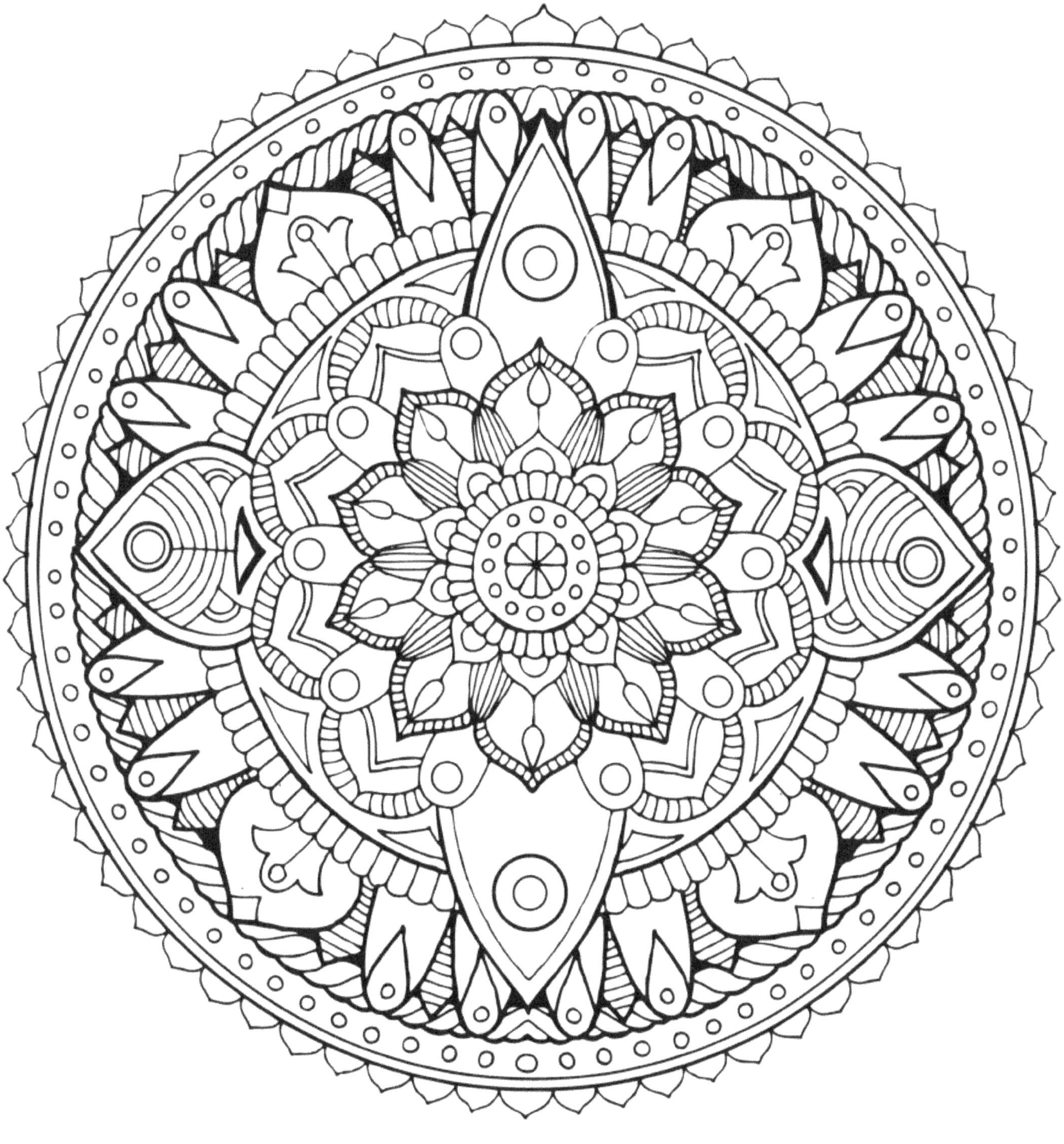

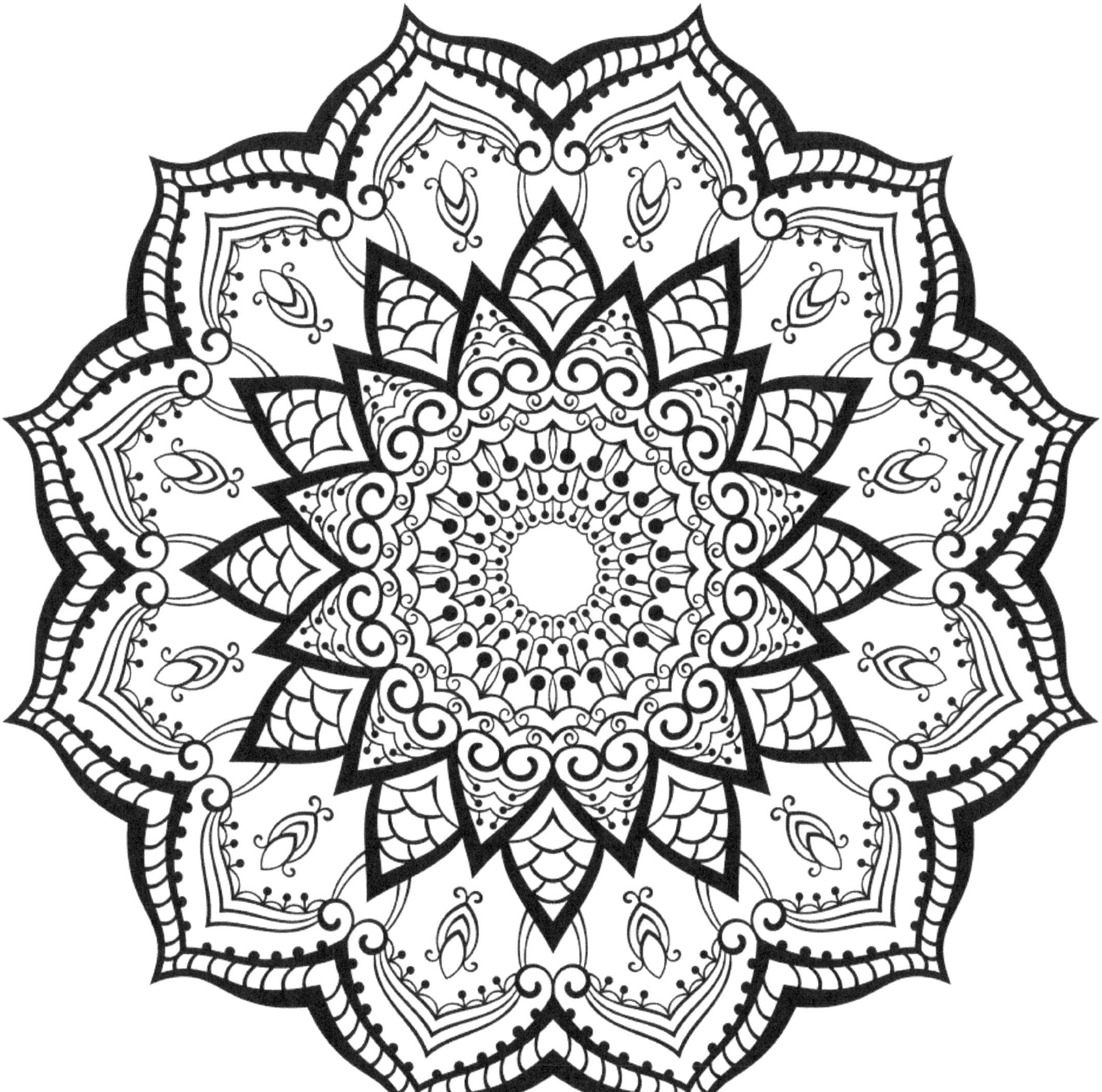

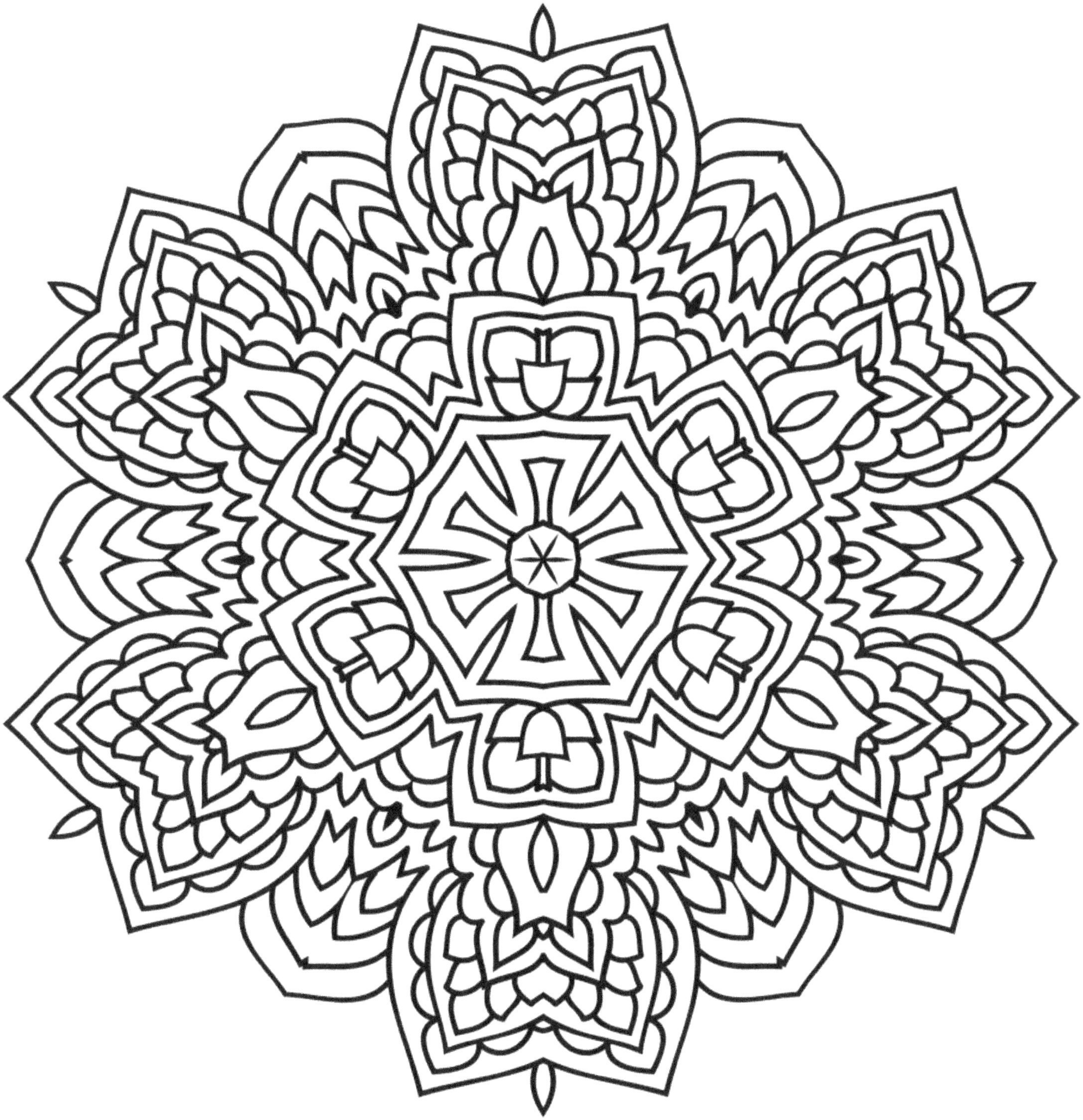

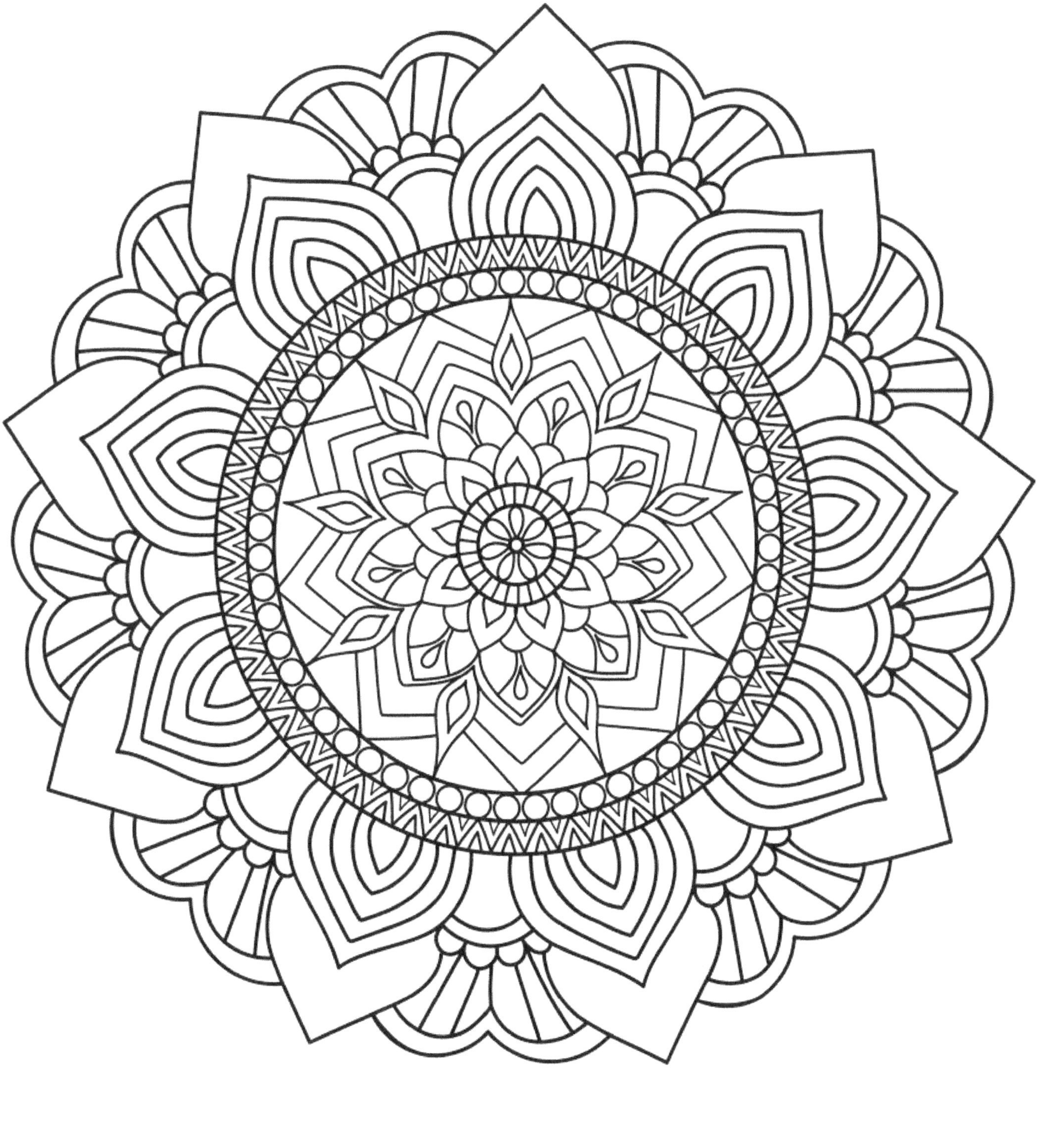

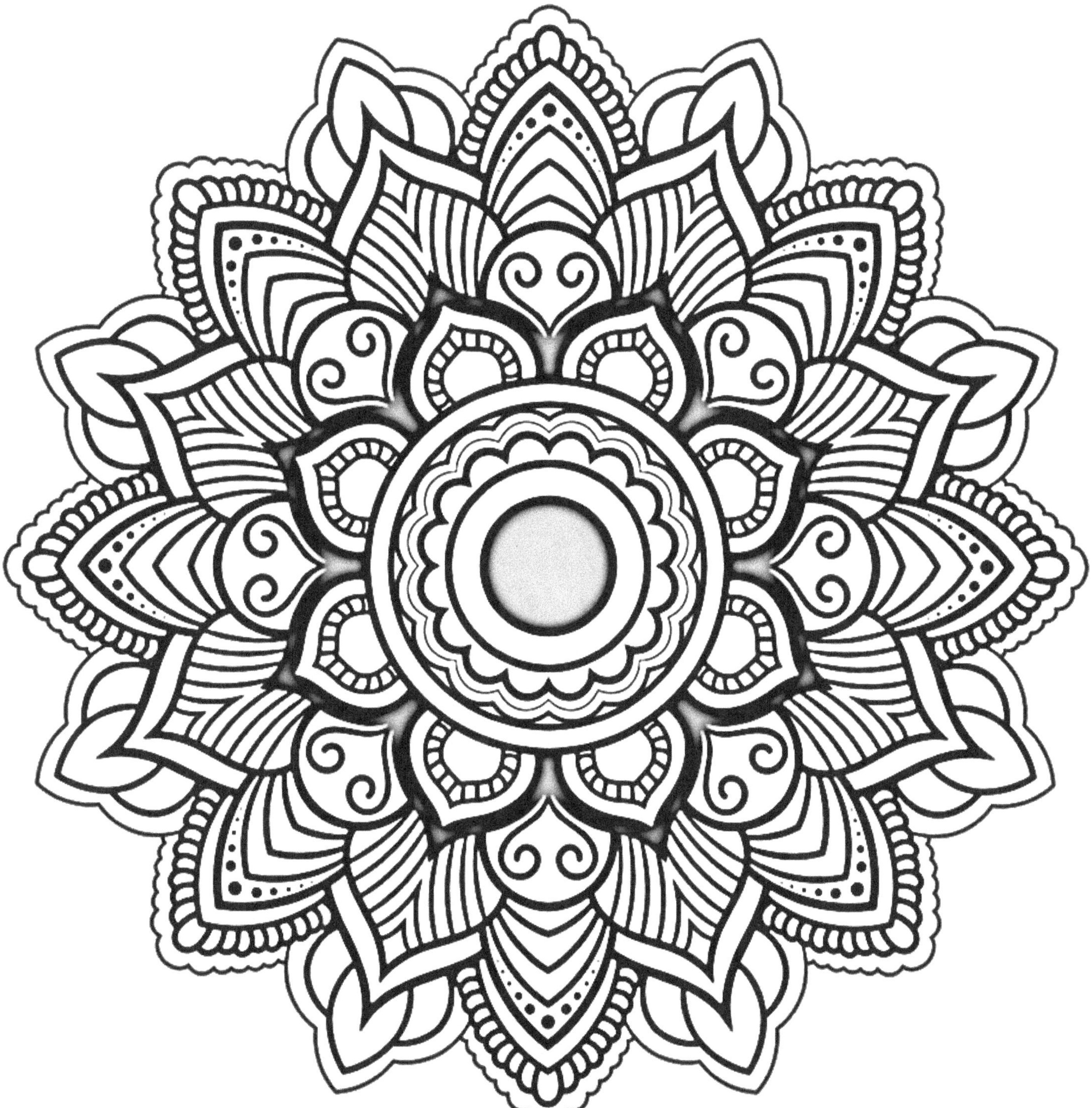

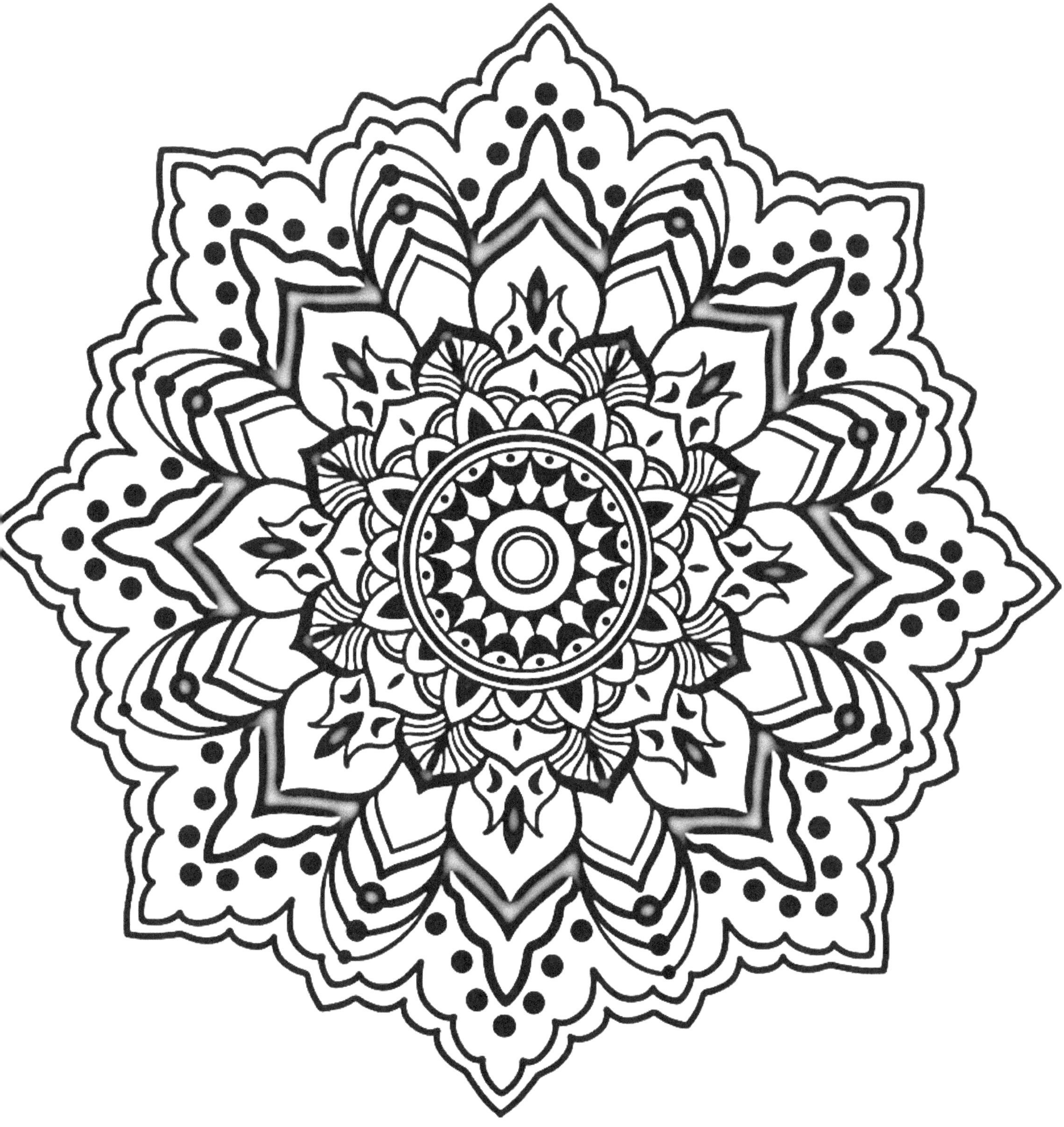

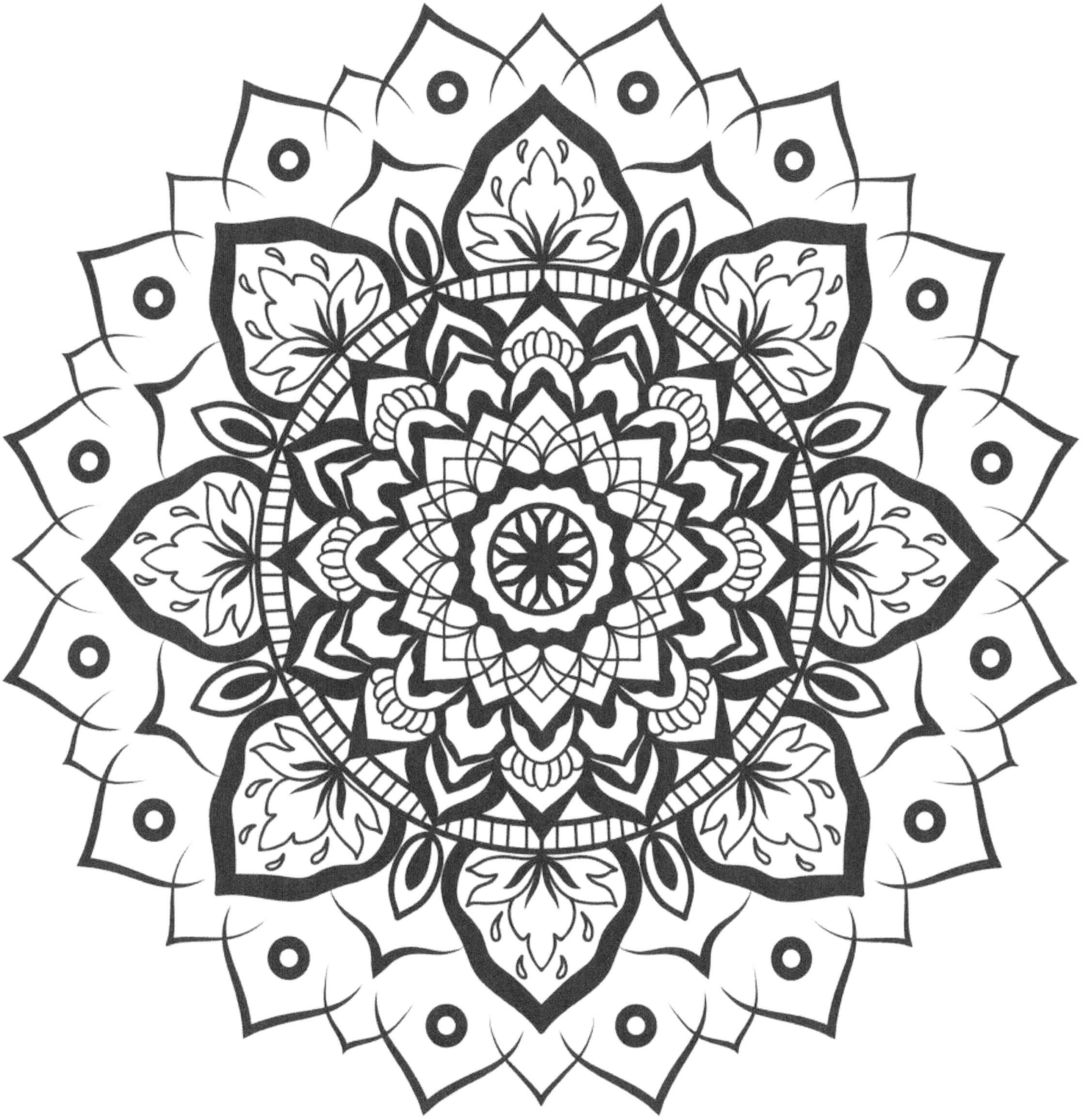

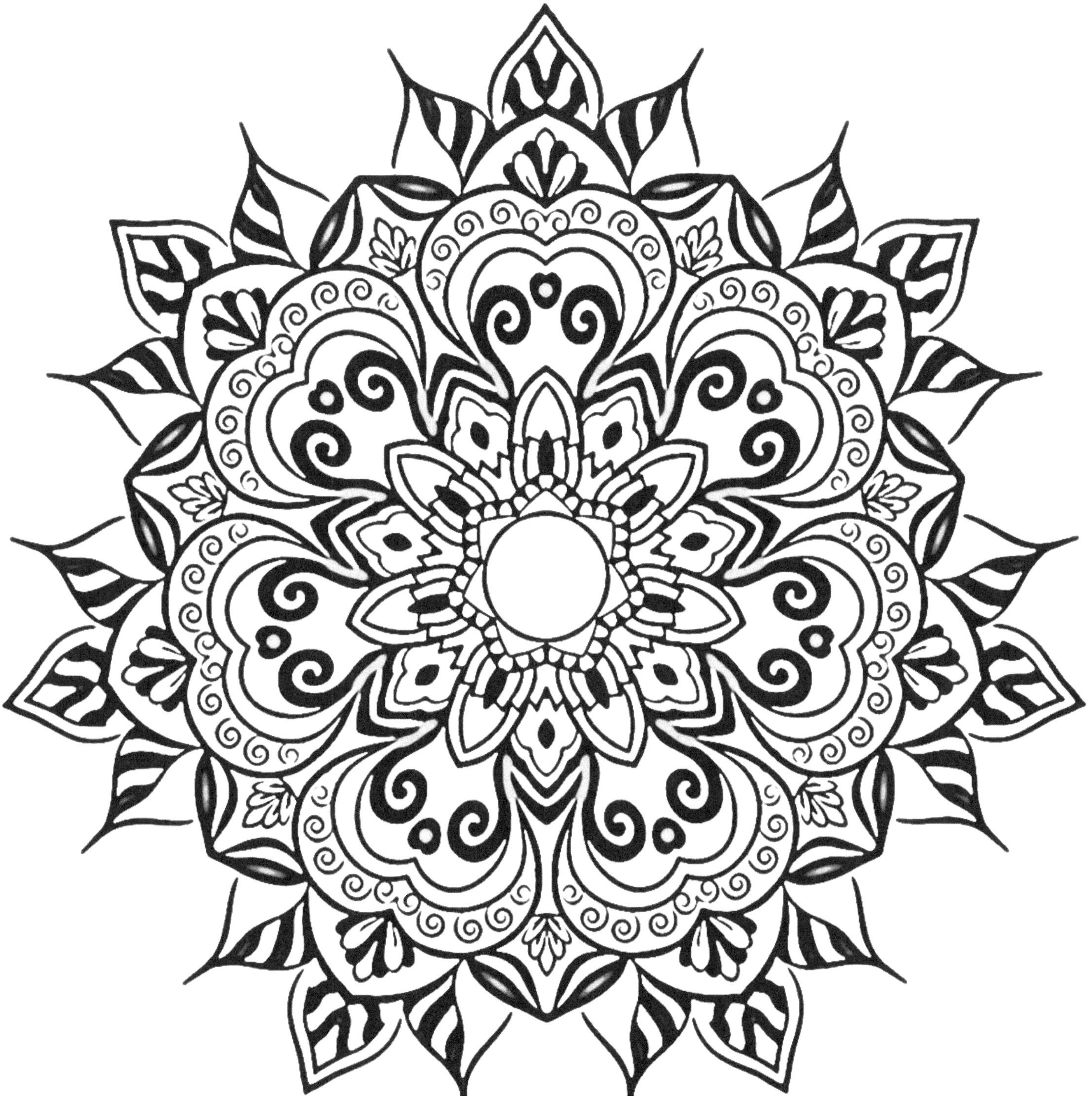

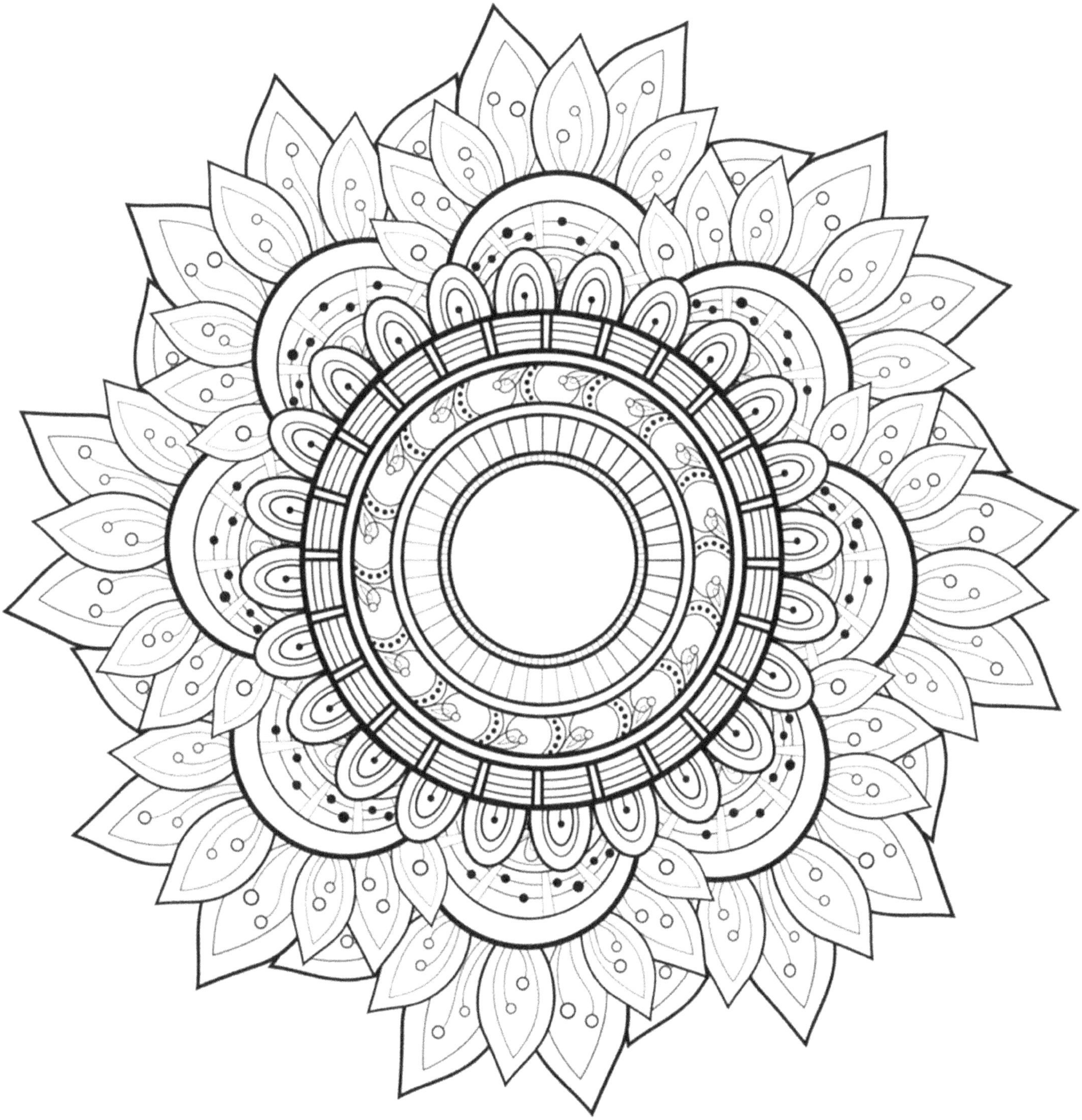

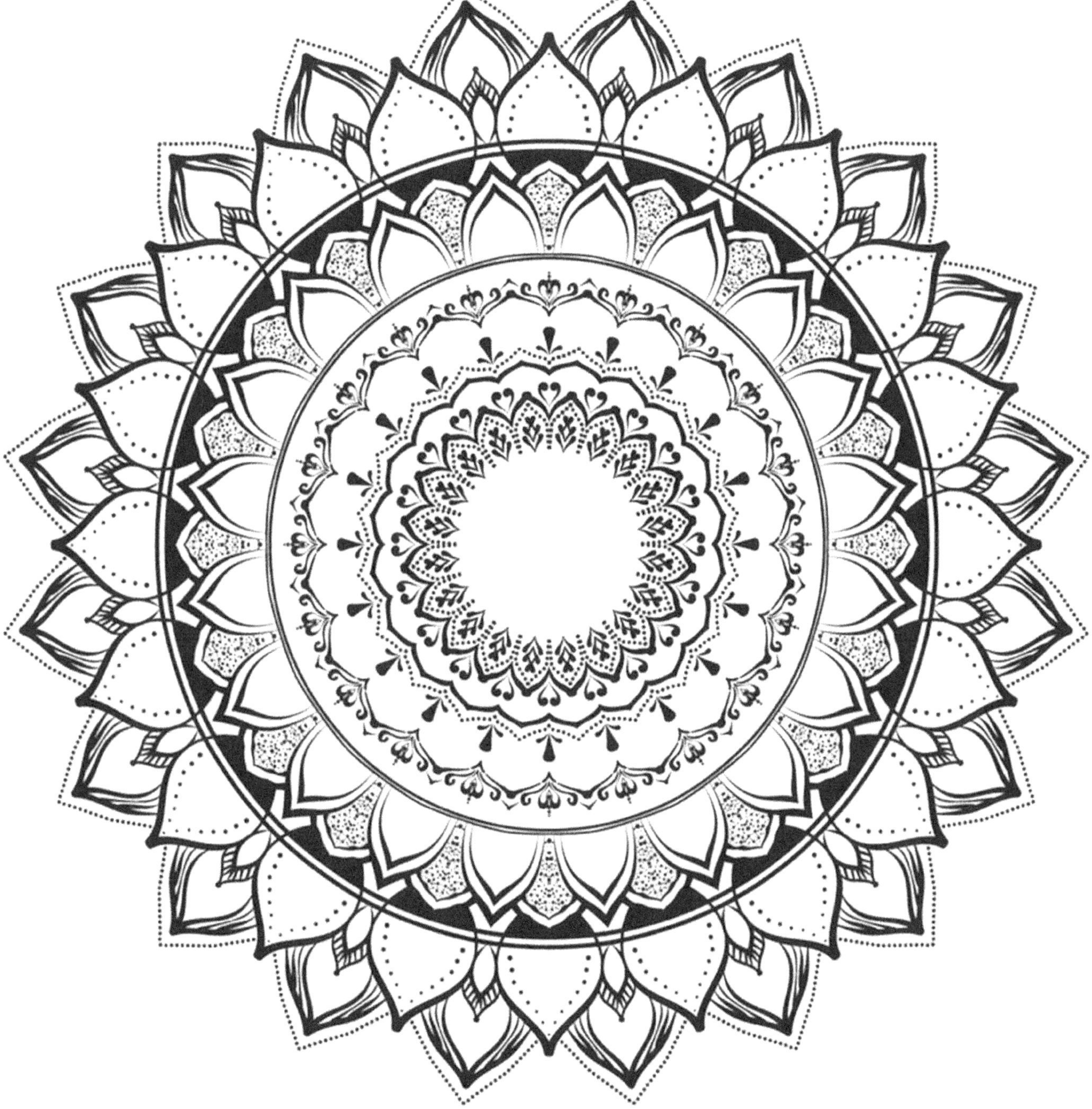

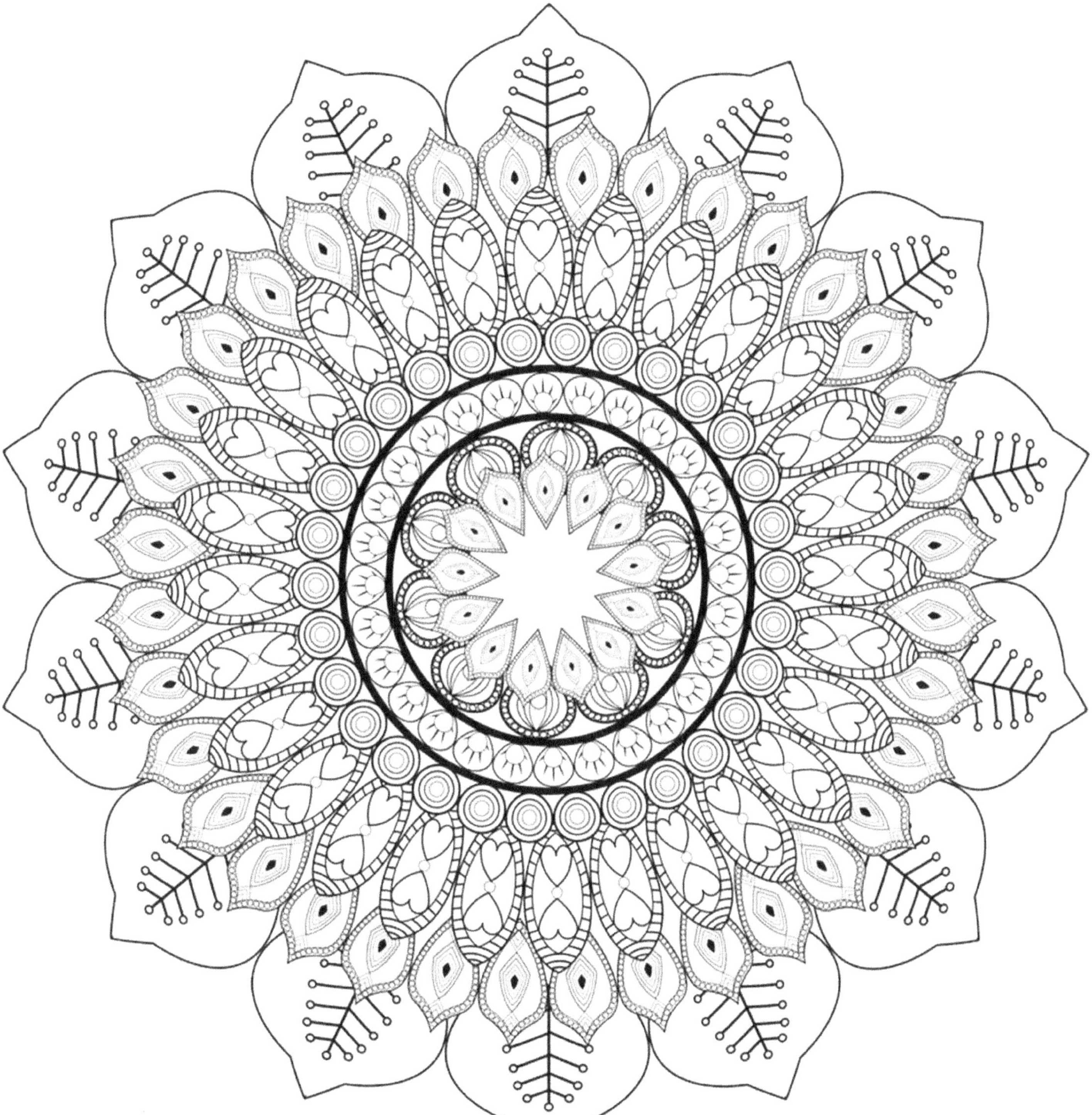

www.ingramcontent.com/pod-product-compliance
Lightning Source LLC
Chambersburg PA
CBHW080856220526
45467CB00008B/2528
* 9 7 8 1 7 1 7 5 3 5 7 4 0 *